THE S.M.A.R.T. ESTATE PLAN

Protecting You and Your Family

JEFFREY L. REHMEYER II

Year of the Book
135 Glen Avenue
Glen Rock, PA 17327

ISBN: 978-1-64649-325-8 (print)
ISBN: 978-1-64649-326-5 (ebook)

Content provided herein is not intended to and does not constitute legal advice or investment advice and no attorney-client relationship is formed. Every effort has been made to ensure that the content is accurate and helpful at publishing time, however, this is not an exhaustive treatment of the subjects. No liability is assumed for loss or damage due to the information provided. You are responsible for your own choices, actions, and results. You should consult your attorney for your specific questions and needs.

CONTENTS

Contents

INTRODUCTION

This book is for you.

This book is for you if you have children.

This book is for you if you don't.

This book is for you if one or more of your children is no longer a minor but now a legal adult.

This book is for you if you might need assistance with your financial or legal affairs someday.

This book is for you if you might need assistance with medical matters someday.

This book is for you if you have parents who might need you for assistance with their financial, legal, or medical matters.

This book is for you if you have pets that you want to see taken care of in your absence.

This book is for you if you want to make gifts to charity and support causes important to you, after you are gone.

This book is for you.

———————✐———————

All of us want to protect the ones we love. All of us want to be able to help our family, should the need arise. All of us will need help at some point in the future.

Accordingly, it is imperative that you plan ahead. Planning need not be difficult or challenging. If you know the right questions to ask, and take the time to answer them, you are well on your way to implementing the kind of planning that can protect your loved ones... and you, should the need arise in the future.

Many people fail to plan, or to even have conversations about their wishes. Because estate planning needs change during different stages of life (new adulthood, moving into married life, growing a family, kids in college, birth of grandchildren, retirement), it's also helpful to review your estate plan when a significant life change occurs.

The sad truth is most adults have not done the proper planning, either recently, or at all.

As an attorney, people contact me to deal with their problems. I can either help them address issues in advance through planning, or I can be involved as an attorney after a problem arises, in which case I attempt to fix it. However, dealing with potential crises in advance, through proven planning, is always a better way to proceed, as it can represent a significant savings in time, worry, and money for you and your loved ones.

I made the realization after law school that my career would revolve around helping other people solve problems. Over the last 27 years, I have received countless telephone calls, emails, and texts during family emergencies. I jump in promptly and try to help. Sometimes it is too late to achieve an optimal resolution, or even a good one. Other times, it is too late to do anything at all. I don't want that to be the case for you.

The purpose of this book is to provide the information you need, in a way that makes legal topics less confusing.

The book is divided into chapters on select topics, so you can focus on those that apply to you now. For example, if you have children under the age of 18, then the planning you need to implement now is different from when your children are adults. Conversely, if you have no children, but have aging parents or others you care about, then you'll want to focus on different chapters. This book is meant to be a resource for today and years to come.

Each topic highlights the questions you need to ask, and will guide you in finding the best answers for your circumstances. Once you answer these questions, the process of implementing an effective plan to protect you and your loved ones becomes much easier.

The stumbling block for many is that they hesitate, sometimes out of fear, and other times because they're unsure of making a wrong choice. Just know that estate planning does not need to bind you for years to come and can be updated at any time. It is far better to make one less than optimum choice, but have an overall plan in place, than to leave your loved ones scrambling when it's too late.

So read on to understand the questions to be asked, the answers that must be provided, the documents to be completed, and other important information that will enable you to protect your family, and yourself, for years to come.

1 THE S.M.A.R.T. ESTATE PLAN

The lessons contained in this book come straight from personal experience helping clients for whom the issues became burdensome. They spent considerable money and emotional energy trying to fix them. The fortunate ones could rectify the problems, but many times the issues could not be resolved.

Before we go any further, let's address that elephant in the room. *Nobody* wants to think about death. Fortunately, you can get the necessary planning done quickly and effectively by answering the right questions.

Everyone is unique, but we share common life events like marriage, buying a house, having children, caring for aging parents, assisting kids through college, dealing with the death of a loved one, and planning for retirement.

All these life changes are important, and most are highly stressful.

I am a husband and a father. I have always done what I could to protect my wife and children. But as kids grow up, protecting them becomes even harder. Plus, the stakes get higher! Small children usually have small problems, but young adults can find themselves in much bigger ones. And nothing is worse than watching your child in pain and being unable to help.

I also assist aging parents and in-laws, and a step-grandmother before she died... In the unfortunate event that something should ever happen to me, I want to know that my loved ones will still be taken care of, and that I haven't left them a mess to sort through to find what they need during their time of loss.

My path to becoming a lawyer, focused on helping others plan for the future, was not a direct one. After high school in central Pennsylvania, I went to the Naval Academy to become a pilot. But then eyesight regulations became more stringent, and I could no longer qualify... so my "vision" of being *Top Gun*'s next Maverick and jetting across the sky was no longer an option.

After that first year at the Academy, I spent the summer on a ballistic missile submarine, the USS Casimir Pulaski.

I still recall "driving" the boat. One midshipman controlled left to right steering while another was in charge of the up and down, seated behind a steering wheel in front of a wall of lights and gauges – obviously with no scenic view.

While off-duty, I exercised on a Lifecycle that was located between missile tubes, listening to Def Leppard, INXS, and Prince on my Sony Walkman. While I tolerated being on the sub, I knew it wasn't my dream job.

So, I returned to the Academy and completed my second year. When my closest friend left and moved to Southern California, he invited me to visit. The invitation was irresistible. I watched a surfing championship in Huntington Beach and went to the Red Onion – a restaurant and night club where my Guess jeans and rugby shirt stood out from others who were more appropriately dressed for KNAC radio's "Heavy Metal Night." I determined that I could work and pay my way through college. So, I packed my 1977 Ford Mustang II (essentially a Ford Pinto) and drove across the country. I cannot imagine what my parents thought.

In California, I became a waiter first, and then a bartender, and worked my way through college at California State University in Long Beach, earning a degree in Economics.

I missed my family, so I returned to Pennsylvania where I became licensed to sell insurance and then became a stockbroker. A couple years later, on the advice of a woman named Margaret who told me in an elegant Southern drawl, "Jeffrey, you should be a lawyer," I investigated law school and applied to the Dickinson School of Law (now Penn State Dickinson), attended for three years and graduated with honors. During the summers of law school, I worked as a law clerk. I passed the Bar Exam, got married, and went on to work at the firm...

But not *The Firm* like the movie. Rather, the CGA Law Firm in York, Pennsylvania, extended an offer when I graduated in 1997, and I've been there ever since.

Initially, I did it all – litigation, family law, school law, business, real estate, plus estate planning. As past president of CGA, I now focus on the latter three and believe estate planning is the best way for me to help people.

Why has estate planning become so important to me? I have seen the pain when people fail to plan.

A friend had an 18-year-old son with a drug problem. One day, his mother found him and had to administer CPR for over 15 minutes until paramedics arrived. They took the young man to the hospital. But because he was 18 and no longer a minor, the mother couldn't be with her son, or even obtain medical updates. In fact, nothing could be done until the young man awoke and gave his consent.

This could have been avoided if they had a Medical Power of Attorney or Advance Healthcare Directive in place.

Some of my clients encountered a similar problem. Their daughter was hundreds of miles away at college in a different state. It was a stressful time for the young woman, as the first semester of college often can be. She suffered a nervous breakdown. Her parents couldn't get information about her condition by phone, so they jumped on a plane. Except once they arrived at the medical facility, their daughter, still distraught and angry, wouldn't grant consent. Days passed before their daughter calmed down and they were even allowed to see her.

These parents felt helpless. They could do nothing to aid their child, now a legal adult. All because important documents were missing.

Many clients in a second or third marriage come to me proactively rather than in a time of emergency. They need help understanding how they can manage their wealth – which includes assets obtained before they were married to each other, as well as those they accumulate together. If something were to happen, they want to take care of each other, but not to the exclusion of their children. These situations require honesty, information, and analysis, but documentation can be created to ensure that all are protected.

These experiences clarified for me the importance of helping others understand how they can protect their loved ones. I came to truly appreciate the questions that need to be asked and answered, and the decisions that must be made.

While the planning process is not always complicated, it can feel challenging to get started. And while the internet might seem to offer answers, the information is often confusing, if not inaccurate.

Proactive guidance and the right counsel are needed. That is why I developed this estate planning program specifically to help you.

Discover how you will:

- **S**et goals and plan for your children and yourself.

- **M**ake sure you can access information and provide assistance to your loved ones when needed.

- **A**bsolve burdens from your children and spouse.

- **R**elieve your family from chaos and confusion.

- **T**ake care of your family in their greatest time of need.

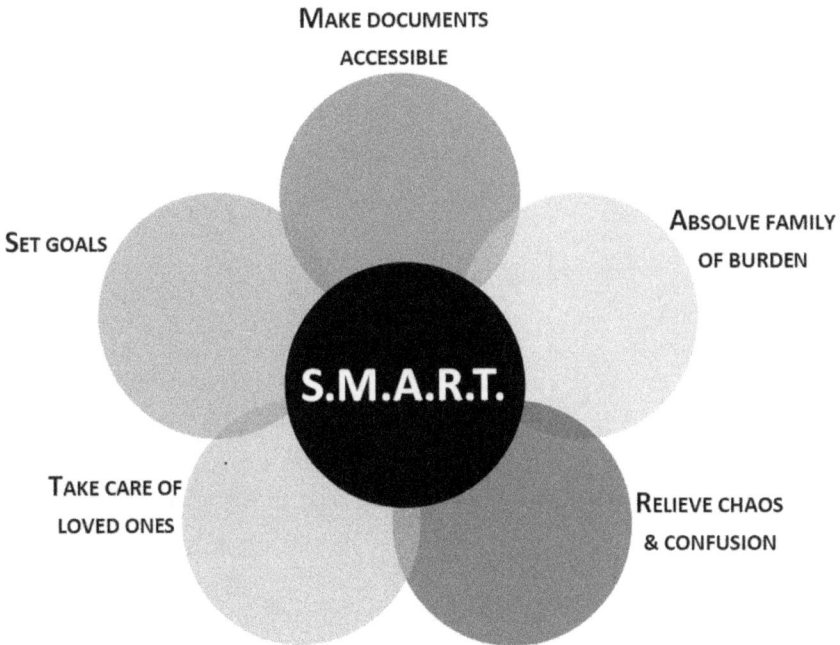

MAKE DOCUMENTS ACCESSIBLE

SET GOALS

ABSOLVE FAMILY OF BURDEN

S.M.A.R.T.

TAKE CARE OF LOVED ONES

RELIEVE CHAOS & CONFUSION

This guide will help you solve problems – legal ones – before they occur.

The first big step is understanding what important decisions you *need* to make. The second is implementing them properly.

It's not your fault. We were never taught any of this in school. There is a lot of confusing information floating around out there. You don't even know what questions to ask. And honestly, most people are approaching it wrong.

So many intend to address these important matters, but find themselves unable to finish, especially on their own. In fact, nearly 70 percent of adults haven't completed the steps, either because of lack of information or fear.

But nothing gets any easier. Plus, laws can be complicated, and are continually changing.

That all ends today.

Let's dive in to the *three* essential documents you need to get started.

2 Essential Documents

There are three main documents, plus one letter, that you and your family members can put in place to alleviate most of the legal difficulties that arise in the event of unforeseen circumstances.

The *Power of Attorney* makes sure someone can access information and provide assistance when needed.

The *Advance Healthcare Directive* allows someone to make critical decisions when a life hangs in the balance.

A *Last Will and Testament* relieves your family from chaos and confusion in your absence. It designates how assets should be allocated, and provides names and direction for those entrusted as Executors, Guardians, and Trustees.

Additionally, a *Final Instruction Letter* alerts your loved ones to the existence and location of all the items they will need to move forward in the days, weeks, months, and years to come.

CRITICAL DOCUMENT #1
POWER OF ATTORNEY

The ***Power of Attorney*** (POA) document designates someone who can make decisions for you when you yourself are unable to do so. A good POA anticipates issues, does not have an expiration date, and will be recognized by others as legitimate under the law because of how it is written and signed.

The POA appoints one or more people to handle financial matters that can include collecting money, paying bills, bringing a lawsuit, and much more.

A POA doesn't always mean the worst has happened. You may simply need help selling a home once you've moved to another state. Or maybe you are away on a long vacation and need someone else to pay bills.

Who should you authorize? Depending on factors like ability and location, a spouse, parents, siblings and even mature children can be options.

Don't Let This Happen to You

Lew's wife contacted me days before he was to have open-heart surgery. They had no planning documents in place. This lack of documentation created uncertainty about Lew's wishes if the surgery did not go well, and the rights of those who could assist him as might become necessary.

PEOPLE INVOLVED

The **Principal** is the person granting the powers to be used.

The **Agent** is the person being granted powers to act on the Principal's behalf.

Powers can be allocated to more than one person, either acting together (both signatures required), or separately (only one or the other signature required).

One or more **Alternates** can be named in the event that the designated Agent is unable to fulfill the role.

Plan Now to Avoid the Chaos

Martin was divorced years ago and recently became ill. He started estate planning but died before he could finish. Now, his affairs are in disarray and his two biological children are not sure what to do because a step-daughter is claiming rights to certain property and investment accounts that she says were "promised" to her. Had Martin completed his planning before he passed, the chaos and confusion could have been avoided.

CRITICAL DOCUMENT #2
ADVANCE HEALTHCARE DIRECTIVE

The *Healthcare Power of Attorney* is a similar document, allowing someone else to obtain healthcare information and make medical decisions when you are unable to do so. The primary difference from a regular POA is that Healthcare POA powers are only exercisable if you are unconscious or incapacitated.

A *Living Will* lets others know your wishes in the event you are in an end-of-life scenario. This can help your family avoid mounting medical bills or eliminate emotional turmoil or court proceedings.

In the absence of these documents, someone has to come forward to be granted authority by the court through a legal proceeding called guardianship, which consumes both valuable time and money.

Together, the *Healthcare POA* and *Living Will* documents are known as an ***Advance Healthcare Directive***.

PEOPLE INVOLVED

The **Principal** is the person granting the powers to be used.

The **Agent** is the person being granted powers to act on the Principal's behalf.

Powers can be allocated to more than one person, either acting together (both signatures required), or separately (only one or the other signature required).

One or more **Alternates** can be named in the event that the designated Agent is unable to fulfill the role.

The concept of a Living Will arose in the 1970s and '80s.

Prior to this time, medical facilities were under obligation to keep people from dying. This directive ignored the possibility that someone might come to be in an end-stage medical condition where a meaningful life is no longer possible.

The courts recognized that appropriate documentation, completed in advance, would allow for the withdrawal of medical treatment and a natural death, without any legal repercussions.

A Living Will now helps families avoid legal controversy, immeasurable emotional pain, and the expenditure of countless dollars and wasted time.

CRITICAL DOCUMENT #3
LAST WILL & TESTAMENT

A *Last Will & Testament* is a written document, signed in the presence of two or more credible witnesses, that stipulates the general distribution of assets upon death. All signatures should be notarized. The person creating the Will must be of sound mind and at least 18 years of age.

A well-written Will identifies the heirs, adequately describes the gifts, and names representatives who will take care of ensuring these requests are followed.

When preparing a Will, consideration should be given to ensure that all individuals nominated to serve as representatives meet any necessary requirements.

A Will may be modified at any time, but must again be signed, witnessed, and notarized, and should designate whether it amends or revokes prior Wills. Ideally, a copy is filed with an impartial third party, like trusted counsel.

"It's really important to not only have a Will, but to also have a conversation with whomever you choose to be in charge of your estate. Let them know why you've selected them, how you would like things to occur, and how you want them to keep peace among the family." —*Bryan Tate, Register of Wills, York County, PA*

PEOPLE INVOLVED

The **Testator** is the person creating the Will, stipulating the distribution of assets after their death.

An **Executor** is a person designated within the Will, chosen to carry out the deceased's wishes.

More than one person can be designated Executor, either acting together (both signatures required), or separately (only one or the other signature required).

One or more **Alternates** can be named in the event that the designated Executor is unable to fulfill the role.

An **Administrator** is someone appointed to carry out the deceased's wishes when an Executor has not been named within the Will.

A **Guardian** is a person designated to provide physical care for children and/or pets.

A **Trustee** is a person designated to administer the wishes of the deceased as expressed through a Trust document.

CRITICAL DOCUMENT #4
FINAL INSTRUCTION LETTER

In addition to implementing the *Power of Attorney*, *Advance Healthcare Directive*, and *Last Will & Testament*, you also need a strategy to consolidate information and have it available if others need to assist.

The ***Final Instruction Letter*** provides such guidance and assembles key information that helps alleviate the chaos and uncertainty for loved ones when they are already heartbroken.

It can include funeral planning details like whether you want to be buried or cremated, have a religious or private service, or have donations directed to a special charity in your memory. It can include information helpful for preparing an obituary, writing a eulogy, or passing on words of wisdom to family.

The *Final Instruction Letter* can also identify people who can help your loved ones deal with the aftermath of your death, like your accountant, life insurance agent, investment advisor, attorney, and employer.

It can also list the location of important papers like titles to vehicles, property deeds, financial statements, and more. When done properly, this document relieves a wealth of stress from your loved ones.

Being smart about your estate planning doesn't have to be painful or prolonged.

You can protect your family by making the necessary decisions now and implementing them through these four critical documents. You just have to follow and complete the required steps.

BONUS

For readers of this book, I offer a special package price for consultation and preparation of all your documents. Receive personal consultation with me, guidance through all the questions to be answered, duplicate originals of all key documents – with one safeguarded on file for you – and the peace of mind that comes from being part of my private client group at CGA Law Firm.

You gain access to nearly 70 professionals who provide legal assistance in Pennsylvania and Maryland, and beyond, in matters involving federal and state law. Obtain legal support for issues involving real estate, business, employment, injury, litigation, and more.

Contact me at:

Jeffrey L. Rehmeyer II
CGA Law Firm
(717) 848-4900 (office)
(717) 718-7115 (direct)
jrehmeyer@cgalaw.com
www.SMARTestateplanbook.com

SET

GOALS

MAKE DOCUMENTS
ACCESSIBLE

ABSOLVE FAMILY
OF BURDEN

S.M.A.R.T.

RELIEVE CHAOS
& CONFUSION

TAKE CARE OF
LOVED ONES

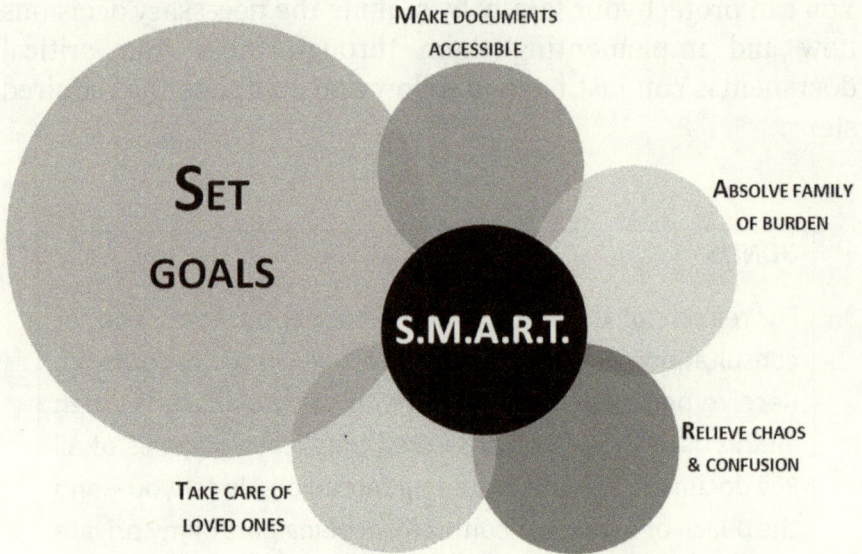

What **GOAL** can you set for this next week or month to move closer to achieving your desire to protect yourself and your loved ones?

☐ Read a chapter related to your family's immediate needs:

- **Chap. 3: Power of Attorney**
- **Chap. 4: Advance Healthcare Directive**
- **Chap. 5: Last Will and Testament**
- **Chap. 8: Death and Probate**
- **Chap. 10: When Your Child Turns 18**

☐ Complete the **Goal Setting** document in Appendix A (page 209).

3 POWER OF ATTORNEY

The first critical document you should have is a **Power of Attorney**. The POA document designates someone who can make decisions for you when you yourself are unable to do so. A good POA anticipates issues, does not have an expiration date, and will be recognized by others as legitimate under the law because of how it is written and signed.

Common uses of the POA include paying bills, collecting money due, filing taxes, or making financial and legal decisions for an aging parent.

A POA doesn't always mean the worst has happened. You may simply need help selling a home once you've moved to another state. Or maybe you are away on a long vacation and need someone else to pay bills.

Who should you authorize? Depending on factors like ability and location, a spouse, parents, siblings, and even mature children can be options.

A POA is typically done as part of the estate planning process. In the case of older adults who may lose capacity at some point, a POA is a more efficient and effective alternative than a legal guardianship proceeding. And while one might assume a POA is *only* important for older adults, it can also be extremely useful for young adults over the age of 18 who are away at college, living at home, or traveling abroad, as once they attain the age of majority, parents no longer have the legal right to make decisions for them.

Let's take a more detailed look at the *Who*, *What*, *When*, *Why* and *How* of Powers of Attorney.

WHO

The **Principal** is the person granting the powers to be used.

The **Agent** is the person being granted powers to act on the Principal's behalf.

Powers can be allocated to more than one person, either acting together (both signatures required), or separately (only one or the other signature required).

One or more **Alternates** can be named in the event that the designated Agent is unable to fulfill the role.

Choosing an Agent under a Power of Attorney requires careful consideration. Choose an individual or individuals who are trustworthy and demonstrate the capability of managing your affairs. Any person may be chosen, including a family member, friend, trusted financial advisor, institution, or professional fiduciary to act in this manner.

When selecting an Agent, consider:

- Trustworthiness
- Financial experience
- Management of personal finances
- Geographic location
- Availability

You may designate more than one Agent. In such case, these people may be empowered to act separately, or be required to act together. If they can act separately, then more than one person has full authority to act with regard to your assets. If they must act jointly, then they need to concur when they proceed, which can often be challenging from a logistical perspective.

CHOOSING A FAMILY MEMBER?

Many people identify a spouse as their POA Agent. Typically assets already owned are held jointly – as *tenants by the entirety*, which means if either one dies, it goes to the other.[1]

For young adults, often a parent is granted POA. For older adults, usually an adult child is named.

For adults whose parents have gotten older, I do see people rely on siblings. Make those decisions based on trustworthiness. Also keep in mind whether the prospective person has adequate financial experience. Someone might be inclined to choose a sibling, but if that sibling is routinely bad with money, this could be a poor decision.

On a personal note, my biological grandmother died of cancer in 1979. Many years later, my grandfather remarried, to a woman named Delores who has four daughters. My grandfather passed away, and Delores began to live with one of her daughters. Over the years, a different daughter died, another retired, and the final daughter had some personal

---

[1] That's the marital equivalent of *joint tenant ownership with right of survivorship*. In the latter case, when there are two or more owners, if one of them dies, their ownership interest goes to whoever is left. This is in contrast to *tenants in common*, where if someone dies, their share is passed on according to directions in a Will or rules of intestacy in the absence of a Will.

issues. Unfortunately, the daughters couldn't agree on how to handle important decisions for Delores's future.

Issues came up. Delores approached me, asking if I would manage bank accounts and pay bills on her behalf as a POA Agent. I had a high degree of devotion to her, so I agreed. I prepared the documents but sent her to another attorney to have them executed. That attorney met with her and evaluated the situation. After discussion, Delores decided to assign financial Powers of Attorney to me, and designated one of her daughters for medical POA (which we will talk about in the next chapter).

Before agreeing to perform as someone's POA Agent, make an attempt to understand what types of issues exist or may arise.

Before agreeing to perform as someone's POA Agent, make an attempt to understand what types of issues may be at play. My step-grandmother's finances were in a state of disarray. Despite owning her condo free and clear, there were real estate taxes and other outstanding bills that had not been kept current. This tanked her credit rating. When there wasn't money to cover large debts, she wasn't eligible for a home equity line of credit, which was very disappointing since she owned an asset worth more than $200k. Making financial decisions on someone else's behalf becomes increasingly complicated when they do not have enough liquid assets to cover routine bills.

MAKE SURE YOU "HAVE THE TALK"

I can't emphasize enough the importance of having open and detailed discussions with the person you choose to assign Powers of Attorney, both at the onset of establishing the POA and afterwards. Neither party will want to be taken by surprise with disturbing facts or become involved in situations that could have been avoided. What could be even worse is for someone to learn they have been assigned Powers of Attorney without their knowledge, and now be forced to serve in a capacity they never envisioned for themselves.

As a matter of law, an Agent under a POA is subject to a number of legal duties. Those duties require certain actions and create potential liability. So before appointing someone, or being appointed, there should be a talk between the Agent and Principal to make sure both parties understand and agree to the responsibility.

It is also important to discuss the logistics of how critical information will be relayed. Will someone deliver bills on a routine basis, or will the person with the POA visit you or some third party to collect these documents? Can online account access and/or automated bill payments be set up to allow easier options? Depending on physical location of all parties involved, these details can be crucial to understand before enacting Powers of Attorney.

Another potential wrinkle is if one person is granted *financial* POA and another *medical* POA. It may be helpful for the person with financial POA to be authorized to access medical information despite HIPAA (Health Insurance Portability and Accountability Act) rules, allowing them to contact hospitals and doctors for information that will help them understand medical bills, follow up with health insurance or Medicare, and make payments as necessary.

Finally, while it is important for you to consider the trustworthiness and potential effectiveness before selecting someone to assign POA, there are also legal requirements that must be met in order to do so.

WHAT

An Agent has three mandatory duties: 1) the duty to act in accordance with the Principal's reasonable expectations to the extent known, and otherwise in that person's best interests; 2) the duty to "act in good faith"; and 3) the duty to act only within the scope of authority granted.

The powers granted can be tailored. Thus, a general POA can include the grant of well over a dozen powers, however, it could be very specific, such as to authorize your Agent to handle a specific financial transaction.

Some powers typically granted include:

- Creating a Trust for your benefit
- Making additions to an existing Trust for your benefit
- Claiming an elective share of the estate of your deceased spouse
- Renouncing fiduciary positions
- Withdrawing/receiving the income or corpus of a Trust
- Conducting real property transactions
- Handling tangible personal property transactions
- Investing in stocks, bonds, and other securities
- Directing commodity and option transactions
- Managing banking and financial transactions
- Borrowing money
- Entering safe deposit boxes
- Buying insurance and investing in annuities
- Handling retirement plan transactions
- Managing interests in estates and Trusts
- Bringing claims or defending litigation
- Obtaining government benefits
- Filing taxes
- Operating a business or entity
- Providing for personal family maintenance

Some powers *not* assigned by a Power of Attorney include:

- Voting in a government election on your behalf
- Consenting to marriage for you
- Performing personal service obligations on your behalf
- Executing a Will for you

There are some other powers that can be *granted only by express authorization*. These powers, known as "Hot Powers," *must* be explicitly written in a financial POA in order for the Agent to exercise them:

- Creating, amending, revoking, or temporarily modifying an *inter vivos* Trust
- Making a gift
- Creating or changing rights of survivorship
- Creating or changing a beneficiary designation
- Delegating authority granted under the POA
- Waiving your right to be a beneficiary of a joint and survivor annuity, including a survivor benefit under a retirement plan
- Exercising fiduciary powers that you have authority to delegate
- Disclaiming property, including a power of appointment
- Accessing your electronic communications and digital assets.

When all of the above powers are granted, the document is often affectionately referred to as the "Blockbuster" Power of Attorney. Many POAs grant an extensive number of powers, because you never know which ones might be needed. But a POA could be tailored, which is commonly done when selling a parcel of real estate for one or more specific purposes.

BEST PRACTICES

An Agent acting on your behalf owes you this duty of care and loyalty. This person must act using due care, competence, and diligence. An Agent who violates the standard of care is liable to you and your successor(s) for the damages. An Agent acting in good faith is not liable for any loss.

> *The Agent must act using due care, competence, and diligence.*

This person must act in accordance with your wishes, to the extent they know your intentions. Otherwise they should act in your best interest.

The Agent must keep records of receipts, payments, and significant actions. They should log all transactions, dates, and third parties involved in the actions. They also must produce an accounting of all transactions if you or another authority requests it.

You may have specific financial goals, such as to pay off all debt or to create a 529 account for grandchildren. There should be regular communication between you and the person you assign POA to allow them to better understand your intentions and desires over time.

It can also be valuable to track conversations by keeping notes. For my step-grandmother, I kept a file with bank statements and bills, and sub-files for key documents like her property deed. When I met or spoke with people about her affairs, I usually took notes of what we talked about.

It may not be necessary to maintain this level of record keeping, but it's always better to have more than you need rather than less.

WHEN

A Power of Attorney may be durable or non-durable.

A *durable* Power of Attorney is effective immediately and remains effective during a Principal's incapacity or disability.

A *non-durable* Power of Attorney terminates when the Principal becomes incapacitated.

By default, Pennsylvania Powers of Attorney are durable, unless expressly stated otherwise.

Generally, the Power of Attorney is valid and in force when signed, but an Agent can't utilize the document without having an original in hand. This becomes a safeguard for you. You can keep the POA document secure until needed, so this power can't be exercised without your consent.

Alternatively, you may choose to make the Power of Attorney effective later, or be triggered by an event such as incapacity or disability.

A Power of Attorney that becomes effective in the future is called a *Springing Power of Attorney*. A Springing Power of Attorney can be beneficial because it can be prepared so that it becomes effective only when you need it. However, the potential downside is that if an event or condition is the trigger, there must also be a method of determining when the event has occurred.

In the case of incapacity, a third party generally must determine when you are incapacitated for the Power of Attorney to become effective. The time it takes to do so might delay the POA from being useful when you need the Agent to act, or may allow for dispute whether the stated event has even occurred. This can frustrate the purpose of the Power of Attorney.

WHY

The Power of Attorney document is frequently utilized because it allows someone to handle the most common financial and property issues.

Let's say you decide to move to Florida. Your Pennsylvania house is on the market after you leave. You don't want to have to fly back for settlement when the sale closes. With a POA, you can authorize this person to handle that sale on your behalf. The POA grants the Agent authority for that transaction, and the POA will also be recorded with the deed and transfer of property.

You may customize the Agent's powers to fit particular needs. From the "What" section above, you may allocate only specific powers as befitting a single situation, or broader powers that can be useful for years to come.

The POA form is frequently used because members of the financial industry know and recognize its validity. There is nothing more frustrating than trying to help a loved one take care of necessary responsibilities, but being thwarted by rules that were set in place to protect individuals in the first place. A third party *must* honor the directions of your Agent acting under a valid Power of Attorney unless the third party has reasonable cause to refuse.

Third parties acting in good faith are exempt from liability when dealing with your Agent appointed by a Power of Attorney. The POA is a means to protect not only you who needs help, but also your Agent who wants to help, and the third party who is legally responsible to you.

Now that we understand the *Who, What, When,* and *Why...* let's talk about the *How.*

HOW – FOR THE PRINCIPAL

LEGAL REQUIREMENTS

The following are requirements for executing the Power of Attorney:

- Have reached 18 years of age

- Have the requisite capacity to execute a Power of Attorney. Having capacity means you can receive and evaluate information effectively and communicate decisions without impairment rendering you partially or totally unable to manage financial resources or to meet essential requirements for your physical health and safety.

- Sign, mark, or direct another individual to sign on your behalf in the presence of two witnesses who are at least 18 years old and are not:
  - The person who signed at your direction
  - The Agent or successor designated in the POA
  - The notary public

- Sign in the presence of a Notary who acknowledges your signature. The Notary may not be a designated Agent under the Power of Attorney.

THE DOCUMENT ITSELF

The Power of Attorney form has *three parts* which include:

- The powers granted by the Principal to the Agent

- A notice to the Principal

- A notice to the Agent

State law requires all three elements to be completed to create a valid Power of Attorney.

On the first page of the document you must acknowledge by signature that substantial powers are being granted. It is important to make sure the person being chosen as Agent is someone who can be relied upon.

At the end of the document, the Agent must acknowledge by signature that actions will be taken in your best interests.

When I work with clients, if they are naming a spouse or an adult child as the Agent, usually we don't need a long discussion. However, it is important to consider the maturity level if selecting a young adult child, or the financial and moral responsibility of any party who may be named as Agent.

Locating a Third Party

I once helped an unmarried woman, Janet, who had no siblings or children. We had to search for a third party whom she could engage to serve as her Agent. Gary was selected. Years later, Janet's mother died. While we were handling the estate, Janet became increasingly absent-minded. So Gary, who was granted Powers of Attorney, was able to assist Janet to administrate her mother's estate, including the sale of a house.

When selecting a third party as Agent, you definitely want to do your research and make sure you are comfortable with their financial and moral responsibility, especially concerning all the powers designated and granted inside the POA document.

While not as common, the use of Powers of Attorney for a child who has reached age 18 can be extremely beneficial for all parties.[2] Many times young adult children need help with something financial. It might feel like common sense that if you are paying college tuition, you should be entitled to information

---

[2] If you have a child nearing the age of 18, we'll cover all of the relevant planning documents in greater detail in Chapter Ten, including what you as a parent need to know to help keep your child safe.

about your child. During orientation days, some institutions offer a form for signature by parent and student that grants parents access to certain financial, academic, and perhaps medical information. However, these powers are of limited duration and are usually tied to the information related only to that institution.

Rather than relying on some blanket form that may or may not exist at your adult child's school, a valid POA will allow you to help when needed as long as the document is in place, either until it's revoked or until the person dies. If the student is attending school in a different state, the POA should be executed within the same state where the student technically resides. We will talk in more detail about this in Chapter Ten.

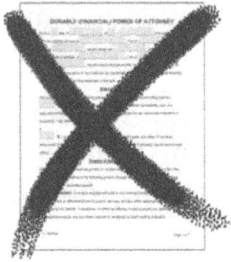

I have not encountered issues where a POA from my firm hasn't been acknowledged in other states, but there are instances where folks simply downloaded a form from the internet or cobbled something together, and the document neither appears formal nor functions legally.

When executed through my law firm, the individual signs the acknowledgment statement and signs the powers granted, which signatures are notarized and then witnessed by two others. The document is in black and white, and the signatures are in blue. There are no stamped signatures.

We create four originals of this document:

One original remains on file in my office, and three are given to the Principal, who may provide one to an Agent, or store them in a safe place if not yet needed.

The POA is most commonly thought of as a need when somebody gets older and requires more help. A lot of older adults list their adult children on their accounts, or grant them signing authority. But in the absence of that, or if something happens quickly like a car accident, the POA allows someone trusted to step in and take necessary action in your best interest when you are unable to do so.

In the event you have not granted POA, but need assistance, the legal proceeding for guardianship can be undertaken. This requires going to court, and you do not get to select the person who will be appointed as Guardian. Instead, this person is chosen by the judge. The process can be lengthy and may require the input of medical experts.

Pennsylvania law allows the Orphans' Court to appoint a *Guardian of the person* (for living arrangements) and/or a *Guardian of the estate* (for financial matters). Anyone interested in a person's welfare can file a Petition seeking a Guardian. But the Guardian must be identified and willing to serve. The Court will not produce a Guardian, and depending on the County, there may be no public Guardian service.

To qualify for a Guardian, a person must be impaired in such a way that they are partially or totally unable to manage financial resources or meet essential requirements for physical health and safety. A ruling of incapacity involves the curtailing of many important rights, and stringent standards must be met. Notice must be given to the alleged incapacitated person and there is a right to request counsel. Moreover, that person will likely be required to attend a hearing before the Orphans' Court unless excused for valid reason, such as by a doctor. When testimony by qualified persons, such as a psychiatrist or other healthcare professional, establishes by clear and convincing evidence that the person is incapacitated, a Guardian will be appointed.

The Guardian of the estate and/or person will be appointed with full or limited powers. It then becomes the duty of the Guardian to assert the rights and best interests of the incapacitated person. If that person has expressed wishes or preferences, they should be followed. A court order is typically very specific about the powers that are or are not granted in the case of a guardianship.

Typical decisions made by the Guardian of the person include arranging medical care and consenting to surgery or other treatments. They also include deciding where an incapacitated person is to live, and even contracting for admission to nursing facilities.

Having someone designated with Powers of Attorney and Healthcare Powers of Attorney is a way to avoid the necessity of guardianship.

REVOCATION

You may revoke a Power of Attorney at any time, but must do so in writing.

Absent revocation, the Agent's authority automatically terminates according to the terms of the Power of Attorney or on the occurrence of certain events, including any of the following:

- The Principal's death
- Incapacity of Principal, if not a Durable Power of Attorney
- Divorce, if the Principal and the Agent were married
- Completion of the Power of Attorney's purpose

If any of the above circumstances apply, the previously enacted Powers of Attorney cease.

HOW — FOR THE AGENT

When you have been granted Powers of Attorney as an Agent, it is important for you to understand how to exercise them properly.

When you utilize POA, typically the bank, financial institution, or entity involved will examine the original notarized document, and then make a photocopy to store in their files. They typically do not keep the original document, which should be held by you for future use. However, in the event that an original document is required, it is helpful to have multiple originals, either in your possession, with the person who granted the POA, or with the lawyer who created the document.

Third parties, such as banks and financial institutions, may accept and rely upon a validly executed POA. However, they may request additional information related to the Power of Attorney:

- An Agent's notarized certification of any factual matter relating to the Principal, Agent, or Power of Attorney

- An affidavit certifying that you did not know of any legal termination of the Power of Attorney at the time you acted

- An English translation of the Power of Attorney (if necessary)

- An attorney's opinion relating to whether you are acting within the scope of the authority granted by the Power of Attorney if the person making the request provides in writing or other record the reason for the request

Powers of Attorney executed in the Commonwealth of Pennsylvania are typically recognized in other jurisdictions. Similarly, Powers of Attorney validly executed in other jurisdictions are recognized as valid in Pennsylvania. However, if a Principal moves from one state to another, it is prudent practice to proceed with a new Power of Attorney in the new state of domicile, written in accordance with its laws.

When acting on behalf of someone else, you as an Agent should sign documents in a certain way: with the Principal's name, your signature, and the designation as Agent.

Sign:	**John Doe by Jane Doe (Agent)**
	Principal's name / Your Name (Agent)

REASONABLE COMPENSATION

Under Pennsylvania law, in the absence of a specific provision to the contrary, you are entitled to reasonable compensation based on the actual responsibilities assumed and performed. Should you decide to claim compensation, you should keep careful records.

I was actually involved in a dispute where one daughter was acting under a Trust and spent hundreds of hours renovating a house. She also involved friends and paid them. When it came time to sell the house, a beneficiary under the Trust challenged her claim for compensation. Because the records were not as detailed, there were numerous questions about whether or not the numbers and compensation amounts were fair. This resulted in a lengthy legal proceeding to resolve the issue.

CAUTIONARY TALES

1 Remember when I said that my firm also maintains one original of the POA? Let's say that you're utilizing Powers of Attorney in a distant state, and a question of legality or legitimacy arises. If an entity is struggling with granting access to the Agent, your attorney can weigh in and substantiate the validity of the legal document. In some instances, I have contacted such institutions as the attorney for the Principal. I explain that the POA was executed in my presence, that it's valid for the purpose being claimed, and is both legitimate and legal.

2 Another reason an original is maintained on file is so if documents get lost, that stored original can be recorded and made of public record. Once the POA is recorded, copies of the recorded document function the same as an original.

3 In an attempt to circumvent the need for a POA, some people list others on their bank account(s). For example, an older parent might decide to have one of his children listed as an owner on his checking and savings accounts. While this may accomplish the desire for someone else to have the authority to make payments or deposits, the downside is that, legally, the child is being given half the value of the account. There can also be tax consequences, and depending upon how the account is titled, if the main account holder dies, the other person could get all of the money.

In a later chapter, we will take a deeper look at how property and assets are treated upon death, either through Probate when a Will exists, or as designated by state inheritance rules. However, it is valuable to note that in the example mentioned above, if the adult child who was added to the account predeceases the father, then the father would be liable for taxes just to get his own money back.

4 Are there fears that after granting durable Powers of Attorney, someone might take actions without your knowledge or approval?

It is possible to create conditions in a POA that must be met before the document becomes effective. Let's say I don't want my POA to be effective until I'm incapacitated. This sounds good in theory, but the problem is that I have to have someone else pass judgment to determine my capacity.

Instead, here's a control mechanism that can be utilized. Most of my clients will keep their original POA documents in their possession, somewhere inside a fireproof box or safe that's readily accessible. If a situation warrants the use of the POA in the future, then the originals can be given to the Agent at that point, or closer to the time when it will be needed.

The Agent does not need to sign the document when it is first created. The Agent can sign the acknowledgment page when later presented with the POA at a date of your choosing. The Agent's signature does not need to be notarized.

5 I caution you against keeping the POA and other important documents in a safe deposit box. Without your presence, someone would need a POA in order to access that safe deposit box. But if the document is inside the box... you see the problem?

In some cases, I have been contacted by the adult children of my clients when something has happened to a parent. I can investigate at that point, and if the claim has merit, I can release the original document.

WHAT AN AGENT CAN'T DO

Under Powers of Attorney, an Agent can't consent for you to be married. The Agent also can't change beneficiary designations on accounts or retirement plans (although it is possible for this to be added to Powers of Attorney if desired and explicitly stated). Under normal circumstances, if a spouse is a named beneficiary, that spouse would be required to sign off, effectively disclaiming property or assets, before an Agent can enact a change of beneficiary.

Disclaiming property is sometimes done as a technique to avoid assets passing in a way that may not be effective. For example, if someone receives public assistance, getting a big financial gift will interfere.

An Agent can't be held responsible for financial actions taken by the Principal. Let's say you're concerned about acting as Agent for someone because of poor decisions that person might make. Your liability as Agent is to the Principal granting you Powers of Attorney, not the other way around. Make sure that whatever document you sign is for Powers of Attorney, as opposed to a different role – like as a guarantor or co-signer, in which case there would be financial responsibility attached.

If you are asked to act as Agent and encounter any red flags, remember that you can always relinquish POA.

It is important to have a discussion between both parties before creating the POA, as to why it's being asked and what is expected. Many times there is a family situation where extraneous members (siblings, aunts, uncles, cousins, adult children) will not agree. This can be particularly challenging and there can be lasting ramifications of choices made.

Also consider whether actions required by the Agent may present any conflicts of interest. For example, if an Agent makes a monetary loan to the Principal who granted the POA, the interest rate should be reasonable and not excessive. If property is being

It is important to have an open and frank discussion between both parties before entering into a POA agreement.

sold, the transaction should be handled in the Principal's best interests rather than those of the Agent. If business contracts are being offered, again, they should benefit the Principal, rather than the Agent, the Agent's spouse, family members, or employer.

Stay clear of anything where either party might get a benefit (perceived or otherwise). Keep a record of all receipts, disbursements, and transactions. An Agent is required to disclose receipts, disbursements, or transactions if ordered by a court, or requested to do so by the Principal, a Guardian or Conservator of the Principal, another fiduciary acting for the Principal, a governmental agency having authority to protect the welfare of the Principal, or an Executor or Personal Representative upon the Principal's death.[3]

Here are some guidelines when acting as an Agent. In addition to duties required under Pennsylvania law, you should:

- Act prudently and reasonably in all actions.

- Avoid conflicts of interest.

- Respect the terms of the document. If you see an ambiguity in the document you should seek assistance.

- Not place any of the Principal's assets in your name.

---

[3] Note: this list does not include the Principal's spouse, children, or heirs.

- Indicate you are acting as Agent when executing documents on behalf of someone else.

- Maintain complete records of all steps taken.

- Keep receipts of checks written and disbursements made. This minimizes the possibility that you will be exposed to liability.

Bryan Tate, Register of Wills, York County, PA

"The best advice I could give is to think ahead years and years. If your family members have to go to court to determine who's going to take care of you because you haven't done that pre-planning for yourself or your family, it's really hard. But if we all just realize that anything could happen in our lives, how much simpler we can make things for ourselves and for our children if we would put some effort into working with a professional and having those documents in place, choosing who we want to take care of us or our children if we're not available to do so."

Power of Attorney is the first of three documents I recommend for your estate planning. In Chapter Four we'll look at the next one – the *Advance Healthcare Directive*, often referred to as a *Living Will*.

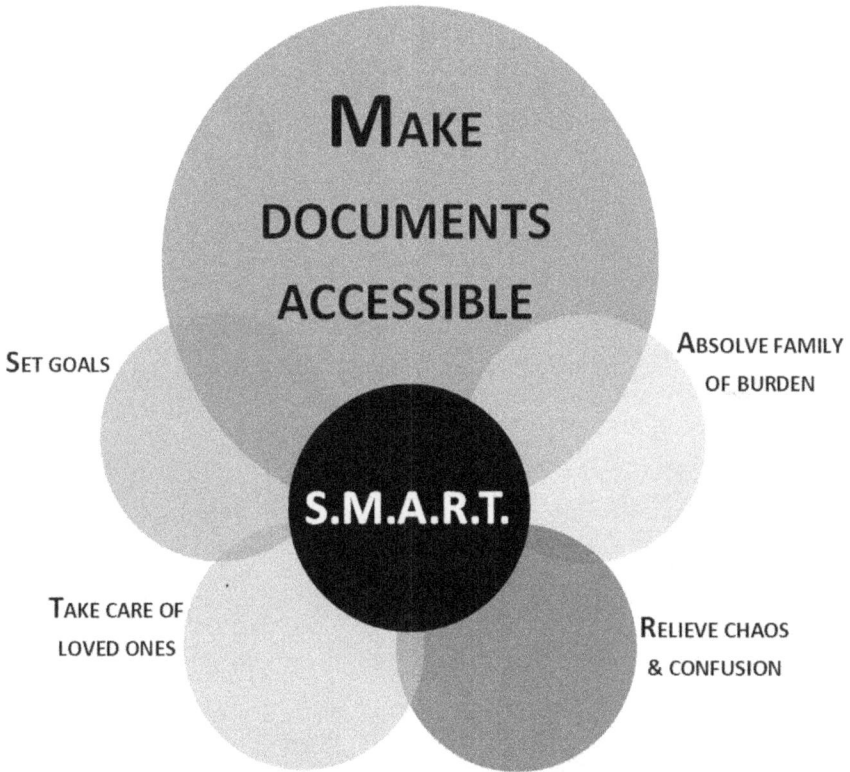

How can you **MAKE DOCUMENTS ACCESSIBLE** for you and your loved ones?

☐ Designate a place in your home to store all your estate planning materials.

- **A physical filing cabinet**
- **A safe (make sure combination is known or accessible)**
- **A drawer or folder**
- **A fireproof box**

☐ Begin to place items in this storage system

☐ Alert family members to this location

4

ADVANCE HEALTHCARE DIRECTIVE

HEALTHCARE POA & LIVING WILL

The second critical document you should have is an **Advance Healthcare Directive**. This is the combination of two important documents: the Healthcare Power of Attorney and a Living Will.

Common uses of the *Healthcare POA* include allowing an Agent to speak with others to obtain information and make decisions on behalf of someone else concerning medical condition, treatment, and care. In the same manner as the Powers of Attorney we detailed in the previous chapter, the Principal is the person who grants powers to an Agent.

In contrast to regular Powers of Attorney, however, this document does not allow the Agent to act unless the Principal is unconscious or incapacitated – meaning a doctor has determined there is insufficient mental capacity to act.

A second manner in which the Healthcare POA differs from the regular POA is that the former concerns medical issues while the latter primarily deals with financial and legal matters.

A *Living Will* lets others know your wishes in the event you are in an end-of-life scenario. This can help your family avoid mounting medical bills and eliminate emotional turmoil or court proceedings.

In the absence of these documents, someone has to come forward to be granted authority by the court through a legal proceeding called a guardianship, which consumes both time and money.

Who should be authorized as Agent for a Healthcare POA? Some prefer that a family member or close family friend with medical training be chosen to serve. Ultimately the selected individual should live nearby and know you well, and of course, respect your wishes and values.

The creation of an Advance Healthcare Directive is often done after seeing a loved one or friend face an end-of-life situation, but because accidents can occur at any time, it is wise to have this document in place before it is medically necessary.

It is also a helpful document to have in place for adult children, because once they attain the age of majority, parents no longer have the legal right to make decisions for them.

Let's take a more detailed look at the *Who, What, When, Why* and *How* of Advance Healthcare Directives.

WHO

The **Principal** is the person granting the powers to be used.

The **Agent** is the person being granted powers to act on the Principal's behalf.

Powers can be allocated to more than one person, either acting together (both signatures required), or separately (only one or the other signature required).

One or more **Alternates** can be named in the event that the designated Agent is unable to fulfill the role.

To execute a valid Advance Healthcare Directive, the Principal must be either 18 years of age or older, a high school graduate, married, or an emancipated minor and be of "sound mind."

COMPETENCY TO MAKE DECISIONS

Under Pennsylvania law, an individual is competent to make healthcare decisions if the individual, when provided appropriate medical information, communication, support, and technical assistance, is documented by a healthcare provider to do all of the following:

- Understand the potential material benefits, risks, and alternatives involved in a specific proposed healthcare decision

- Make that healthcare decision on their own behalf

- Communicate that healthcare decision to any other person

A healthcare decision is one regarding an individual's medical care, including, but not limited to the following:

- Selection and discharge of a healthcare provider

- Approval or disapproval of a diagnostic test, surgical procedure, or program of medication

- Directions to initiate, continue, withhold, or withdraw all forms of life-sustaining treatment, including instructions not to resuscitate

- Admission to a medical, nursing, residential, or similar facility, or entering into agreements for the individual's care

- Making anatomical gifts, or after the death of the individual, disposing of the remains or consenting to autopsy

An individual can be competent to make some healthcare decisions, but not others. If the competency of a Principal is in question, an attending physician should perform a capacity evaluation and enter a determination of incapacity into the medical record.

If you as the Principal are determined to be incompetent, an Agent must make a healthcare decision in accordance with your individual healthcare instructions, if any, and any other wishes to the extent known to the Agent. Otherwise, that person must make the decision in accordance with their determination of your best interests. In determining your best interests, the Agent must consider your personal values, to the extent known.

If you have not appointed an Agent and are not competent to make healthcare decisions, Pennsylvania law provides an order of priority for who may act as your healthcare representative and make healthcare decisions. A healthcare representative generally has the same authority as a healthcare Agent appointed under an Advance Healthcare Directive.

If you have not designated a healthcare Agent and there is a need for someone to make healthcare decisions on your behalf, then the court may appoint a Guardian. A court-appointed Guardian may make different decisions for you than you would for yourself.

In cases where there is a signed Advance Healthcare Directive and a Guardian has been appointed, the Advance Healthcare Directive – including both the Living Will and Healthcare Power of Attorney – remains a binding legal document, even after you become incapacitated.

CHOOSING AN AGENT

When choosing a healthcare Agent, you should carefully consider options and choose someone with whom you can place your trust. The Agent should:

- Know you well

- Respect your objectives and values

- Live nearby

- Agree to act as your Agent

Some clients prefer to choose a family member with medical training, for example, a registered nurse or medical doctor. Medical training is not necessary, however, but it may be helpful and should be considered when selecting someone to serve in this way. You should discuss the role with them before executing the Healthcare Power of Attorney. You should also confirm the nominated person is:

- A competent adult

- Available if you cannot make healthcare decisions

- Willing to act according to your wishes

- Able to handle potential family conflicts regarding your wishes

You may designate multiple alternate Agents. Those persons may be allowed to act individually. You may also designate multiple Agents to act together. In that case, they would all need to authorize every action. This can be cumbersome and could create a stalemate if they cannot agree.

MAKE SURE YOU "HAVE THE TALK"

I can't emphasize enough the importance of having open and detailed discussions together, both at the onset of establishing an Advance Healthcare Directive and afterwards.

A discussion of various medical treatments that you *would* and *would not* want under certain conditions is critical, as is your decision regarding the application of life-sustaining apparatus.

The person acting on your behalf should also be knowledgeable about your desire regarding organ donation.

Having advance knowledge of your wishes can relieve the burden for someone left to make difficult choices in a traumatic situation. Additionally, in the event of family disagreement, such discussion prior to the life-threatening situation can make all the difference.

WHAT

The *Healthcare POA* enables you to grant authority to someone else to communicate with others and make decisions about your medical condition, treatment, and care.

The person you name as Agent must act in accordance with your instructions. Unless you expressly limit the Agent's powers, this person will have authority to:

- Make healthcare decisions for you to the same extent as you could if competent

- Authorize admission to a medical, nursing, residential, or similar facility and enter into agreements for your care

- Make certain decisions regarding anatomical gifts

- Dispose of remains

- Consent to an autopsy

- Authorize the release of your records to the extent necessary for the Agent to fulfill duties

The *Living Will* section of an Advance Healthcare Directive provides an individual with the opportunity to maintain autonomy regarding medical treatments when diagnosed with a terminal condition or if the individual is in a persistent vegetative state.

Pennsylvania recognizes the right of individuals to make decisions regarding their own medical care, including the decision to receive, withhold, or withdraw life-sustaining procedures.

The use of this portion of the Advance Healthcare Directive may help to:

- Answer difficult questions regarding your preferences for death and dying

- Reduce family arguments

- Avoid unwanted and unnecessary medical care and expense

- Provide peace of mind for you and family members

Treatment that can be withheld as part of the Living Will includes:

- Cardiopulmonary resuscitation (CPR)

- Intubation (mechanical respiration)

- Artificial nutrition and hydration (feeding tube)

- Antibiotics

Comfort is prioritized, so pain relief is often provided, even if it could hasten death.

ORGAN DONATION

The Pennsylvania Department of Transportation has partnered with the Department of Health in cooperation with the Center for Organ Recovery and Education (CORE) and The Gift of Life Donor Program in an effort to promote organ and tissue donation awareness. Donation is strongly encouraged and voluntary.

When applying for or renewing a Pennsylvania driver's license or identification card, an individual may choose to have the "Organ Donor" designation printed on the card. This distinction may also be included in the Healthcare POA and Living Will documents.

While working with clients **Russell and Janet Miller of Hanover**, ages 95 and 93 respectively, Russell did not feel he could be an organ donor because his hearing and eyesight were failing. *"Nobody would want any of my organs,"* he said.

In actuality, there are still many useful organs that can be donated to help others live better quality lives. The oldest organ donor on record was 95.

Donations can include kidneys, liver, lungs, heart, pancreas, intestines, hands and face, corneas, middle ear, skin, heart valves, cartilage, tendons, ligaments, bone, veins, stem cells, and bone marrow.

Thousands die every year waiting for a donated organ. When just one person signs up to be an organ and tissue donor, they can potentially save up to eight lives through organ donation and enhance the lives of 75 others through tissue donation.

The disappointing truth is that only a very small percentage of all designated organ donors ultimately achieve this goal because of conditions relating to the time and place of death, or the lack of immediate access to facilities to harvest organs.

Most frequently, organ donation happens after a situation in which the mind is not functioning but the body is still alive or being kept alive.

Missy Sweitzer Slenker
Mother who lost her 20-year-old son

"Zachary was our first child. He was on his way home from his girlfriend's house when an impaired and fatigued driver hit his truck. Unfortunately, my son did not have a seat belt on and was ejected as a result of the crash. He suffered a traumatic brain injury. We got that call that no parent ever wants to get.

Zachary was in the hospital for three days and never regained consciousness. He was declared clinically and legally brain dead. When the subject of organ donation came up, I knew that it wasn't our decision.

Zachary chose to be an organ donor. When we were at the DMV, and as a mom of a minor I had to sign off. I said, 'Buddy, do you want to be an organ donor?' He was like, 'Duh, Mom. Why wouldn't I? If something ever happens to me, give somebody else a chance.'

I am so grateful that he made that decision and made us aware of it, because that took one less thing off of us. That was honestly a relief to us.

Unfortunately, only 2.5 percent of patients who die are eligible to give life-saving transplants. Even though a person might be a registered donor, they have to die in a specific manner in which to be able to donate organs. So many people are currently awaiting transplants."

WHEN

An Advance Healthcare Directive (including Durable Healthcare POA and Living Will) is an important document for any adult, regardless of age. It allows an individual to make decisions about how he or she will be cared for, and it provides guidance for loved ones.

It comes into use when a person is in need of care but is unable to make critical decisions. This can be useful for older adults or for parents of children who have reached 18 years of age. But because accidents can happen at any time, it is always better to be prepared in advance.

For a Living Will to come into play, the person needs to be unconscious, but an alternate trigger is an irreversible coma or a persistent vegetative state, though these states may come hand in hand. When the body is dying, often the mind is not functioning either.

In contrast, let's say someone is diagnosed with cancer. That person is still alive and functioning at the outset. They are not in a scenario where the Living Will is involved. At least not early on. This person can still make decisions about treatment independently.

Receiving such a diagnosis, however, acts as a cue for many to finally take action at creating a Healthcare POA and Living Will.

If a person with an end-stage medical condition recognizes that an incident might trigger medical care but they know that, even if revived, they wouldn't continue with a reasonable quality of life, a Do Not Resuscitate order (sometimes referred to as a DNR) informs paramedics or other medical staff as to whether resuscitation is desired by the patient.

A DNR can be in the form of a written order, bracelet, or necklace, the contents of which are described by applicable law. They are intended to direct emergency medical service providers to comply with wishes not to be resuscitated when experiencing cardiac or respiratory arrest and have both the healthcare directive and an out-of-hospital DNR issued in accordance with the law. The EMS provider can withhold CPR upon observing such a DNR order, thus following the patient's wishes.

DNR orders are often implemented by individuals who recognize that if they face a substantial health crisis, they may not have the quality of life to which they want to return, and thus do not believe that resuscitation is necessary.

A Physician Order for Life-Sustaining Treatment ("POLST") form has been approved by the Commonwealth of Pennsylvania.

The use of a POLST is intended to help ensure that a patient receives appropriate care at the end of life. This is achieved by creating an actual medical order that directs care consistent with the patient's goals and preferences, while at the end of their lives.

The form can transfer with the patient when moving between medical providers, such as being transferred from a hospital to a nursing home. The POLST gives the patient choices that include a full range of care options, from aggressive to limited to comfort care. Seriously ill patients, or their Agent under a Healthcare Power of Attorney, should discuss these options with healthcare professionals so they can be appropriately documented.

The POLST is different from a Living Will or Healthcare Power of Attorney in that it is an actionable medical order dealing with the current medical situation and thus more readily applicable if circumstances warrant.

People don't generally make a DNR or POLST without receiving some critical diagnosis. When you enter most medical facilities for treatment, or any place that might put you under anesthesia, they will ask if you have completed an Advance Healthcare Directive, DNR, or POLST, and if so, they will want to review it so they can act in accordance with your wishes if necessary.

AT THE CARE FACILITY

Dr. Michael Spangler of UPMC Memorial in York, PA, explains that the original document of an Advanced Healthcare Directive should be brought to the facility by the patient or family. That original is then scanned into the hospital's electronic record-keeping system.

When the patient's chart is accessed, a notification sidebar comes up, warning that the patient has an Advance Healthcare

Directive on file. Dr. Spangler recommends patients bring the document with them for any initial or substantive visit. In case of critical medical conditions, a "Living Will is the most powerful document that you can have in your possession," he advises.

FOR ADULT CHILDREN

When children turn 18, a parent is no longer able to legally make decisions for the child. An Advance Healthcare Directive is a great way to ensure that loved ones will be taken care of in the event of an accident.

I recently assisted one of my daughter's high school friends to create her documents. She's 22 and her parents are divorced. As is often the case, a parent was the one who prompted the discussion and paid for the documentation. In this case, the mother was selected as Agent, with an uncle as alternate. Ultimately, it's the Principal's choice.

I provide the client's parents with a copy of the document to review and share with their child beforehand. When we meet I then typically ask follow-up questions to ensure understanding.

For this document to become valid, you need to be physically present for the notarization of the Advance Healthcare Directive. In December 1999, the Uniform Electronic Transactions Act was passed in Pennsylvania, allowing for electronic signatures to be valid on some document types, whether fax or e-mail, but two areas still require live signatures – those are estate planning documents and real estate documents.

While live signatures are required, remote online notarization offers a way to complete the process without a notary needing to be physically present. Signing is done via video and the notary's stamp is electronic.

While this is now possible and used if needed, typically people prefer a face-to-face meeting with a traditional notary process and traditional in-person signing.

WHY

Advance Healthcare Directives arose late last century as a result of a number of cases involving the "right to die." The first such case ever heard by the United States Supreme Court was *Cruzan v. Director, Missouri Department of Health*, which was decided on June 25, 1990. In a 5-4 decision, the Supreme Court affirmed the earlier ruling of the Supreme Court of Missouri and ruled in favor of the State of Missouri, finding it was acceptable to require "clear and convincing evidence" of a patient's wishes for removal of life-support. A significant outcome of the case was the creation of the Advance Healthcare Directive, which could be that clear and convincing evidence.

KAREN ANN QUINLAN

A well-known case involves Karen Ann Quinlan. When she was 21, Quinlan became unconscious after she consumed Valium along with alcohol while on a crash diet and lapsed into a coma, followed by a persistent vegetative state. Quinlan had suffered irreversible brain damage after experiencing an extended period of respiratory failure (lasting no more than 15-20 minutes).

The Quinlans filed a suit on September 12, 1975, to require that the extraordinary means prolonging Karen Ann Quinlan's life be terminated. New Jersey's Superior Court Judge rejected the request, as doing so would violate New Jersey's homicide statutes.

The Quinlans appealed the decision to the New Jersey Supreme Court, which granted their request, holding that the right to privacy was broad enough to encompass the Quinlans' request on Karen's behalf. When Karen was removed from the respirator/ventilator in May 1976, she surprised many by continuing to breathe unaided.

Karen Ann Quinlan's parents never sought to have her feeding tube removed. "We never asked to have her die. We just asked to have her put back in a natural state so she could die in God's time," Julia Quinlan said. Karen was moved to a nursing home and was fed by artificial nutrition for nine more years, until her death from respiratory failure on June 11, 1985.

NANCY CRUZAN

On January 11, 1983, then 25-year-old Nancy Cruzan lost control of her car while driving at night. She was thrown from the vehicle and landed face down in a water-filled ditch. Paramedics found her with no vital signs, but they resuscitated her. After three weeks in a coma, she was diagnosed as being in a persistent vegetative state. Surgeons inserted a feeding tube for her long-term care.

Years later, in 1988, Cruzan's parents asked her doctors to remove her feeding tube. The hospital refused to do so without a court order, since removal of the tube would cause Cruzan's death.

The Cruzans filed for and received a court order for the feeding tube to be removed. The trial court ruled that constitutionally, there is a "fundamental natural right . . . to refuse or direct the withholding or withdrawal of artificial death prolonging procedures when the person has no more cognitive brain function . . . and there is no hope of further recovery." The court ruled that Nancy had effectively "directed" the removal of life-support by telling a friend earlier that year that if she were sick or injured, "she would not wish to continue her life unless she could live at least halfway normally."

The state of Missouri and Nancy's guardian *ad litem* (the person appointed by the Court to look out for Nancy's best interests) appealed the decision. In a 4-3 decision, the Supreme Court of Missouri reversed the trial court's decision. It ruled that no one may refuse treatment for another person, absent an adequate Living Will, "or the clear and convincing, inherently reliable evidence absent here." The Cruzans appealed and in 1989, the Supreme Court of the United States agreed to hear the case, which was then argued on December 6th of that year.

The legal question decided by the Supreme Court was whether the state of Missouri had a right to require "clear and convincing evidence" for the Cruzans to remove their daughter from life-support. Specifically, the Supreme Court considered whether Missouri was violating the Due Process Clause of the 14th Amendment by refusing to remove Nancy's feeding tube. The Due Process Clause provides "[N]or shall any State deprive any person of life, liberty, or property, without due process of law."

The Cruzans' lawyer summarized the constitutional basis for the appeal as follows:

> *"The issue in this case . . . is whether a state can order a person to receive invasive medical treatment when that order is contrary to the wishes of the family, when it overrides all available evidence about the person's wishes from prior to the accident, when the decision to forego treatment is among acceptable medical alternatives and when the state gives no specific justification for that intrusion other than their general interest in life.*
>
> *We submit that the Fourteenth Amendment and the liberty guarantee there protects individuals, conscious or*

> *unconscious, from such invasion by the state, without any particularized interest for that invasion."*

In a majority opinion by the Supreme Court, Chief Justice Rehnquist ruled that competent individuals have the right to refuse medical treatment under the Due Process Clause. However, with incompetent individuals, the Court upheld the state of Missouri's higher standard for evidence of what that person would want if able to make their own decisions. This higher evidentiary standard was deemed constitutional.

TERRI SCHIAVO

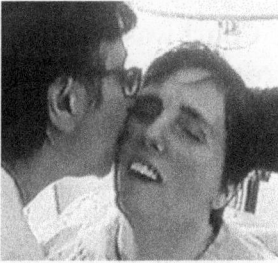

An additional right-to-die case was that of Terri Schiavo. At the age of 26, Terri sustained a cardiac arrest in her home in Florida on February 25, 1990. She was successfully resuscitated, but had massive brain damage due to lack of oxygen to her brain, and was left comatose. After two and a half months without improvement, her diagnosis was changed to that of a persistent vegetative state. For the next two years, doctors attempted therapy of various types. In 1998, Schiavo's husband petitioned the Sixth Circuit Court of Florida to remove her feeding tube pursuant to Florida law. Terri's parents, Robert and Mary Schindler, opposed.

The Schiavo case ultimately involved 14 appeals and numerous motions, petitions, and hearings in the Florida courts, five suits in federal district court, extensive political intervention at the levels of the Florida state legislature, Governor Jeb Bush, the U.S. Congress, and President George W. Bush, and four denials of *certiorari* from the Supreme Court of the United States. The case also spurred highly visible activism from the pro-life movement, the right-to-die movement, and disability rights groups.

Notably, Terri did not have a Living Will. Accordingly, the cases were initiated to determine what Terri's wishes would have been regarding life-prolonging procedures. During those cases, there was substantial question about Terri's capacity.

Terri Schiavo has been compared to Karen Ann Quinlan and Nancy Cruzan. However, the Schiavo situation became a series of cases and they involved settled law rather than breaking new legal ground on the right-to-die issues.

How – For the Principal

Legal Requirements

An individual of sound mind may make a Living Will governing the initiation, continuation, withholding, or withdrawal of life-sustaining treatment if the individual:

- Has reached 18 years of age

- Has graduated from high school

- Has married, or is an emancipated minor

The document must be dated and signed by you or by another individual authorized to do so on your behalf.

The document must be witnessed by two individuals, each of whom is 18 years of age or older. An individual who signs a Living Will on your behalf may not also witness the Living Will.

Additionally, a healthcare provider or its employees may not sign a Living Will on your behalf if the individual provides healthcare services to you.

The Document Itself

The standard *Healthcare POA* form contains a number of checkboxes including questions about organ donation. The Agent may make those decisions on your behalf until you reach a point where the Living Will would come into play, during end-of-life scenarios.

A Healthcare POA may, but need not:

- Describe any limitations you impose upon the authority of the healthcare Agent.

- Indicate your intent regarding the initiation, continuation, withholding, or withdrawal of life-sustaining treatment.

- Indicate whether you want tube feeding or any other artificial or invasive form of nutrition or hydration.

- Request that the healthcare Agent exercise their sole and absolute discretion to consult your relative, cleric, or physician should they be uncertain of your wishes or best interests.

Unless otherwise specified, the Healthcare POA becomes operative when:

- A copy is provided to the attending physician; and

- The attending physician determines that you are incompetent.

The *Living Will* document contains a number of checkboxes for critical decisions. The specific directives of these checkboxes are only implemented *if* someone is in an end-stage medical condition, permanently unconscious, or in an irreversible coma.

I do ( ) do not ( ) want the attending physician to withhold or withdraw life-sustaining treatment that serves only to prolong the process of my dying, if I should be in a terminal condition or in a state of permanent unconsciousness.

I direct that treatment be limited to measures to keep me comfortable and to relieve pain, including any pain that might occur by withholding or withdrawing life-sustaining treatment.

In addition, if I am in the condition described above, I feel especially strong about the following forms of treatment:

- o I ( ) do ( ) do not want cardiac resuscitation.

- o I ( ) do ( ) do not want mechanical respiration.

- o I ( ) do ( ) do not want tube feeding or any other artificial or invasive form of nutrition (food) or hydration (water).

- o I ( ) do ( ) do not want blood or blood products.

- o I ( ) do ( ) do not want any form of surgery or invasive diagnostic tests.

- o I ( ) do ( ) do not want kidney dialysis.

- o I ( ) do ( ) do not want antibiotics.

I realize that if I do not specifically indicate my preference regarding any of the forms of treatment listed above, I may receive that form of treatment.

Other instructions:

- • I ( ) do ( ) do not want to designate another person as my surrogate to make medical treatment decisions for me if I should be incompetent and in a terminal condition or in a state of permanent unconsciousness. Name and address of surrogate (if applicable). Name and address of substitute surrogate (if surrogate designated above is unable to serve).

- • I ( ) do ( ) do not want to make an anatomical gift of all or part of my body, subject to the following limitations (list as desired).

When an Advance Healthcare Directive is executed through my law firm, you sign the document, then your signature is notarized and witnessed by two others. The document is in black and white, and the signatures are in blue. There are no stamped signatures.

We create four originals of this document:

One copy remains on file in my office, and three are given to you. You may choose to provide one to an Agent, or store all the originals in a safe place if not yet needed.

Some elderly people post their Living Will document in a highly visible spot within their home. This can be helpful to family members or close friends who have been enlisted in times of crisis. The downside of such a storage method is that paramedics or others may not see it. They are focused on saving your life and preventing death. Even in the emergency room, doctors have a duty to prolong life. It's only after you get beyond the emergency room and have been stabilized, to whatever extent possible, that there comes a deeper evaluation of the condition of body and mind.

REVOCATION

You may revoke a Healthcare POA or Living Will at any time and in any manner, regardless of your mental or physical condition. The revocation of a Healthcare POA or Living Will is effective by way of communication to the healthcare provider, by either you or a witness to the revocation. Unless your Advance Healthcare Directive expressly states otherwise, it remains in effect until revoked by you.

HOW – FOR THE AGENT

If you have been granted Healthcare Powers of Attorney as an Agent on someone else's behalf, it is important for you to understand how to exercise them properly.

Have a frank discussion of various medical treatments that the Principal who is granting these powers would and would not want under certain conditions, as well as that person's decision regarding the application of life-sustaining apparatus.

The Living Will identifies end-stage medical conditions that can result in death despite the introduction of any treatment. According to Dr. Michael Spangler of UPMC Memorial in York, PA, treatment designated as "futile medical care" – meaning it won't make a difference to the patient's outcome – is a distinction made by the care provider and can be a bit of a wild card. When you are an Agent, understanding the wishes of the Principal is critical as this person has placed you in a position of trust.

CAUTIONARY TALES

1 When my mother-in-law's cousin's husband died, she was in my office the very next Monday morning wishing to update her documents. It's surprising how quickly people want to update documents after a relative or friend dies. I've come to believe that updating documents is a natural part of how many deal with death.

In addition to death, if you see someone start to lose the ability to speak or feed themselves or breathe independently, it can prompt you to question decisions you would prefer if you should ever be in similar circumstances.

2 Don't think you have to name all your children as Agent for Healthcare Powers of Attorney, which could make it cumbersome for any or all to act. Consider how well they get along, and where they live geographically. Balance your desire to include everyone with how their interaction might actually play out. Serving in this capacity is likely more of a burden and a duty than a reward.

Remember, you can pick one child as Agent and then name one or more alternates. Or you could pick two or more who may act separately or together. In the case of multiple children being selected and required to act together, it can be difficult to achieve timely notice and consensus if they do not all live locally.

3 Consider choosing a POA who has some level of financial experience as they may be called to deal with matters pertaining to medical bills for healthcare providers, hospitals, and medical equipment.

Dr. Michael Spangler, VP Medical Affairs
UPMC Memorial Hospital, York, PA

On Medical Powers of Attorney...
"Make sure to pick someone who's going to be actively involved. It is so important for your POA holder to know exactly how to reach the attending physician. They should be having daily or even twice a day discussions, understanding what the goals of care are, understanding where the patient is now versus tomorrow or three days from now. That sets the stage for communication. The doctor knows that your POA knows what's going on, and the POA is constantly informed of those small wins and losses. I think that's where the gray zone ends up becoming clarity."

On the Living Will...
"Just because the Living Will says you don't want to be intubated, it does not mean that the minute you hit the emergency department that all bets are off. We will do what we need to get you better. The Living Will is really reserved for end-of-life decisions when chronic medical conditions aren't getting better."

MAKE DOCUMENTS
ACCESSIBLE

SET GOALS

ABSOLVE

FAMILY OF

S.M.A.R.T. **BURDEN**

TAKE CARE OF
LOVED ONES

RELIEVE CHAOS
& CONFUSION

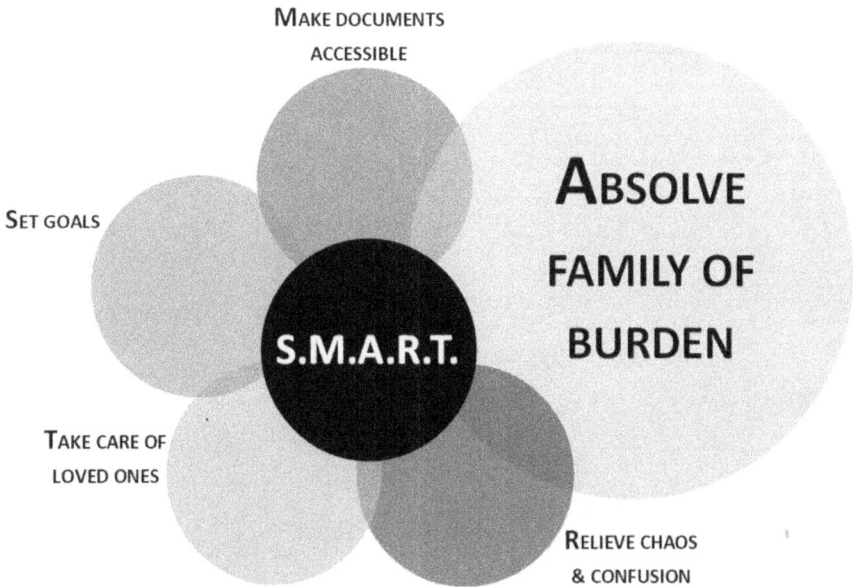

How can you **ABSOLVE FAMILY OF BURDEN** at a time that will already be stressful?

☐ Consider who to select as **Agent** for granting **Powers of Attorney.**

☐ Complete the **Living Will** portion of the **Estate Planning Questionnaire** in Appendix B (page 211).

☐ Contact trusted counsel to set an appointment to create these documents.

5
LAST WILL AND TESTAMENT

A **Last Will and Testament** is a written document that stipulates the general distribution of assets upon someone's death. The person creating the Will must be of sound mind and at least 18 years of age. The document must be signed and witnessed by two others, with all signatures notarized.

A well-written Will identifies the heirs, adequately describes the gifts, and names representatives who will take care of ensuring these requests are followed.

A Will may be modified at any time, but must again be signed, witnessed, and notarized, and should designate whether it amends or revokes prior Wills. Ideally, one original Will is kept in a secure location. For my clients, I retain that original Will in a locked, waterproof cabinet. Copies of this document are provided to clients and key loved ones.

In many states, when someone dies without a Will – known as dying *intestate* – the State determines who receives the property, in what order, and in what shares. If no heirs can be located, then the State receives the property.

This uncertainty can be avoided through the preparation of a Will, and does not need to be overly complicated, though as you will see, there are many options for customization based on asset allocation and personal wishes.

Let's take a more detailed look at the *Who, What, When, Why* and *How* of a Last Will and Testament.

WHO

The **Testator** is the person creating the Will, stipulating the distribution of assets after death. This person must be at least 18 years of age and of sound mind. The term **Testatrix** can be used to refer to a female who creates the Will.

An **Executor** is a person named within the Will, designated to carry out the deceased's wishes. The term **Executrix** can be used to refer to a female Executor.

More than one person can be designated **Executor**, but they both must act together on key issues. (Both signatures required.)

One or more **Alternates** can be named in the event that the designated Executor is unable to fulfill the role.

An **Administrator** is someone designated to carry out the deceased's wishes when an Executor has not been named within the Will.

A **Guardian** is a person designated to provide physical care for children and/or pets.

A **Trustee** is a person designated to administer the wishes of the deceased as expressed through a Trust document.

TESTAMENTARY CAPACITY

To make a valid Will, you must have *testamentary capacity* at the time it is executed. For that, you must be at least 18 years of age and of sound mind. But what does "of sound mind" mean?

Soundness of mind requires that you know, at the time the Will is executed:

- The general composition of the estate

- How the estate should be divided and distributed upon death

- The heirs or other people to be included as beneficiaries

If one of these elements is missing, you do not have the capacity to make a valid Will.

Generally, less capacity is required to execute a Will than to conduct ordinary business affairs. A person can have testamentary capacity *even if* they:

- Are old with untidy habits, partial memory loss, inability to recognize acquaintances, or incoherent speech

- Are confused, eccentric, and unable to manage business affairs

- Occasionally have memory lapses

- Have a medical diagnosis of late-stage dementia five days before executing the Will

- Are adjudicated mentally incompetent within weeks after executing the Will

Evidence of testamentary capacity must relate to a time at, or near, the execution of the Will. If your capacity is questionable, it is a good practice to draft a letter or note creating a record that:

- Discusses your testamentary capacity

- Outlines what questions were asked to determine testamentary capacity

- Memorializes your responses and the steps taken to ensure that testamentary capacity requirements were met

CHOOSING AN EXECUTOR/EXECUTRIX

The Executor/Executrix of an estate is the person who is responsible for collecting assets, paying creditors, selling property if necessary, and making distributions to the beneficiaries. When creating a Will, this is generally the last choice to be made as it comes at the end of the document, even after Guardians and Trustees.

In Pennsylvania, an Executor *may not* be:

- Under 18 years of age

- A corporation not authorized to act as a Pennsylvania fiduciary

- A person (other than an Executor designated in the Will) that the Register of Wills finds to be unfit

- The nominee of any beneficiary or heir of the estate when the beneficiary or heir is outside the United States

- Any person who is charged with voluntary manslaughter or homicide (except homicide by vehicle relating to the decedent's death)

When selecting an Executor, consider someone who is honest, trustworthy, conscientious, capable of remaining impartial, and both available and willing to serve.

In some situations, rather than designating a family member or friend to serve as Executor, it may be better to nominate a third-party who can act impartially according to your wishes.

When a Will does not nominate an Executor, or none of the persons nominated can serve, the Register of Wills grants letters appointing an Administrator in the following order of priority:

- To those entitled to the residuary estate under the Will

- To the surviving spouse

- To those entitled under intestate law to receive the estate assets as the Register determines will best administer the estate, giving preference to the sizes of the share

- To the deceased's principal creditors

- To other fit persons

- To the nominee of the person renouncing the right to letters of administration

- To the guardianship support agency serving as Guardian of an incapacitated individual who dies during the guardianship

- To a redevelopment authority formed under the Pennsylvania Urban Redevelopment Law

For estates where there was no Will, or the Will was proven invalid, the Register grants letters of administration in this same order of priority.

Difficulties of Naming More than One Executor

Curtis died within two weeks after getting married. His Will named his brother and his new wife Co-Executors, but they don't trust each other.

Curtis's brother was not a beneficiary of any real substance under the Will, but his new wife is, so the brother has less incentive to maximize gifts to the beneficiaries. He does stand to recover a commission for serving. He lives in Michigan and the wife lives locally, so he is neither as available nor as effective in the role, which is frustrating to the wife.

At the time of death, Curtis and his brother each owned half of a property inherited from their father – a farm appraised at over half a million dollars. The brother had a right to purchase Curtis's half of the farm so he could own the whole thing, but faced a conflict of interest. As a buyer, he wanted to minimize the purchase price, but as Co-Executor, he was duty bound to obtain as much as he could.

While it is absolutely possible to name multiple Executors in an estate, this is a cautionary example of how conflicting interests, lack of trust, and differing amounts of availability and effort can sow seeds of discord among family during already trying times.

Compensation

Appropriate compensation provisions should be included in the Will. Pennsylvania law allows an Executor to receive *reasonable compensation*. But keep in mind that this compensation may be subject to income tax, whereas amounts inherited under the Will may not.

If the Executor is also a beneficiary of the estate, it might be appropriate to include a provision in the Will stating that the Executor will serve without compensation. Even without this provision, in most circumstances, the Executor can still renounce compensation if desired.

Waiving Bond

To protect the beneficiaries of the estate, Pennsylvania generally requires an Executor to post bond as security for the estate assets. However, the heirs may unanimously agree that the named Executor is trustworthy. In this case, the Court may determine that a bond is not required.

Alternatively, it is common practice to include a provision in the Will waiving the bond requirement unless there is a specific reason for concern. Even if the Will waives the bond requirement however, some Courts may still require it before granting letters of administration.

Savvy Tip: If you're named as an Executor, you really should insist on a face-to-face meeting to talk about the assets, wishes, and relevant family matters (or perhaps more importantly, the family dynamics) of the person naming you in the Will. Serving as an Executor can be a substantial amount of work. Do your future self a favor by having an important conversation and understanding where to access needed information in the event that you are required to act.

CHOOSING A GUARDIAN

Guardianship gives legal custody of a minor child, the minor's estate (that is, the minor's assets), or both, to the appointed Guardian. For a parent with minor children, this is generally the most important issue in the estate plan.

Guardianship provisions are not likely to be needed unless both parents die while the child is still a minor. However, they should be included in the Will in the unlikely event that both parents die simultaneously or too close in time for the surviving parent to update their own Will.

At the time a named Guardian petitions the court for guardianship, the Guardian *must not be*:

- Under 18 years of age

- A corporation not authorized to act as fiduciary in Pennsylvania

- A parent of the minor, except if appointed Co-Guardian with another

Predicting all of the needs of a child (or children), and naming a Guardian(s) who has the ability to meet all of those needs should both parents die, is nearly impossible.

Consider someone who can be trusted both morally and financially to make good decisions. Ideally this person will share similar parental values.

A Guardian must have time to do all the things normally taken care of by a parent.

Time should also be a factor. A Guardian would need to do all the things a parent normally does, including transporting children to sports and other extracurricular activities, and attending events like back-to-school nights and parent-teacher conferences.

A lot of people will pick siblings or friends, but bear in mind that if friends already have four children of their own and you have three, even if they're willing and a good fit, supporting a family with seven children will trigger different financial needs – like new housing, and a much bigger vehicle.

Give thought to choosing someone with whom the child will be most comfortable, bearing in mind that proximity matters. For example, my brother was never listed as a Guardian for my kids because he lives in Boise, Idaho, and would not relish moving back to York, Pennsylvania, to take care of my children... and my children would not have enjoyed moving to Boise for him to take care of them.

CHOOSING A TRUSTEE

Trustees are responsible for administering any Trusts created under the Will. The Executor or Administrator makes distributions from the estate to the Trustee in accordance with the Will provisions. The Trustee also may collect assets, such as proceeds from life insurance policies, when the Trust is named directly as beneficiary. The Trustee must administer the Trust for the beneficiary according to the terms set out in the Will.

When considering the nomination of Trustees, remember the time involved. Whereas an Executor's role may conclude within several months or a year, a Trustee's role can last for many years.

Nominating the same person as Executor and Trustee may make sense in certain circumstances and can aid in a seamless transition from the estate to a Trust. However, some people prefer one person to serve as Executor of the estate and another person or entity to serve as Trustee, retaining the power over long-term Trust investment and distribution decisions.

For example, a close family member may serve as Executor to ensure that key decisions immediately after death are made by family, while a corporate Trustee steps in for long-term financial management of Trust assets.

> *Whereas an Executor's role may conclude within months, a Trustee's role can last for many years.*

Either way, a Trustee should be trustworthy, have the necessary skills to carry out required duties, and have no inherent conflicts with the beneficiaries.

Trustees must administer the Trust in good faith and are generally held to the prudent investor rule, however the Trust instrument may alter or eliminate the prudent investor rule and provide its own standards for managing and investing Trust assets that will override the statutory standard.

WHAT

One of the primary functions of a Last Will and Testament is naming the beneficiaries who will receive assets upon your death. This can include parents, siblings, a spouse, children, grandchildren, great-grandchildren, nieces and nephews, and friends, as well as charitable organizations.

The Will can also identify who will deal with death expenses, as these can become deductions for purposes of inheritance tax.

When preparing a Will, you may make various types of bequests, detailed below. Bear in mind that the Will provisions only control probate assets.[4] Common asset types include real estate (unless owned under an LLC or other entity), personal property (such as a car, art, jewelry, firearms, collections, musical instruments, and antiques), intellectual property (patents, registered trademarks, books, music compositions), and business interests.

Gifts named in the Will can be either:

- Specific or general items such as real property, tangible personal property, and cash

- Residuary gifts (what is left over after expenses are paid and specific and general gifts are made)

Requests for bequests can also be made in the Will, called *precatory* requests, that are not necessarily binding on the Executor but do give some insight into the deceased's intentions.

---

[4] Items like life insurance policies and retirement accounts typically have named beneficiaries designated directly within those documents, and therefore are non-probate assets that do not flow through the Will. These designations supersede any designations in the Will.

Not all gifts designated by Will are guaranteed to succeed. A gift may fail because the named item no longer exists, or the beneficiary has already died, or there are insufficient assets in the estate. Gifts must be analyzed in conjunction with current assets and long-term plans, and of course, can and should be revisited over time to assure they are still accurate and fulfilling your intentions.

SPECIFIC AND GENERAL BEQUESTS

Specific bequests are gifts of specific items of property, such as "my diamond necklace." These may include real and personal property and gifts of cash in specified accounts.

General gifts or "legacies" are gifts that do not direct delivery of any particular property. These can be of a certain dollar amount or value, and may be satisfied out of the general assets of the estate.

Both specific and general gifts have potential downsides, however. Specific gifts are limited to the item described in the Will, so if that item is no longer owned at the time of death, the beneficiary will not receive that specific item or anything in its place.

In the case of general gifts – specifically named sums of money – the overall value may have become reduced due to inflation as the years pass. If you would like a gift of a specific dollar amount to keep up with inflation, inflation-indexing language should be included in the Will. Thus a gift determined today will have the same buying power in the future.

Planning documents often fail to adequately identify property to be gifted, resulting in unintended or adverse consequences.

Why does it matter how a gift is described? The language is applied to property owned at the time of death, which could cause desired gifts to fail or to impact other gifts.

Language that works:

> "I give my sixteen-inch gold necklace with the blue sapphire to my granddaughter Sophia, provided that I still own such necklace at the time of my death, otherwise this gift shall lapse."

If you have the necklace when you die, then Sophia receives it. If you sell or give it away prior, then there is no such gift for Sophia.

Problem language:

> "I give 1000 shares of Apple stock to my son, Todd."

If you have the shares when you die, then Todd gets them. If you don't have the shares, then your Executor could be forced to spend estate monies to buy 1000 shares to make the gift to Todd. But what if you die without enough assets to buy the shares? A gift such as this would create serious challenges with unintended results.

REAL ESTATE

A specific gift of real estate can be made either outright or in Trust. The description of the property in the Will should include sufficient information to identify it clearly. To avoid uncertainty, the legal description of the property or the parcel identification number assigned by the county map office can be included.[5]

If the property is left to more than one person, the Will should specify whether the beneficiaries will own the property as tenants in entirety, joint tenants with right of survivorship, or as tenants in common. If the Will does not specify, the law

---

5 In Pennsylvania, this information can be found on the tax assessment office website for the county in which the property is located.

presumes a tenancy by the entirety for married couples, and otherwise a tenancy in common.

If the property is encumbered by a note or mortgage, you should consider how the debt will be taken care of. Will it be paid off by the estate before passing, or will the beneficiary become responsible for this?

Absent a provision to the contrary in the Will, the beneficiary inherits the real property subject to any associated debt.

Consider how any mortgage or lien against a property will be paid, as well as required taxes.

The Will should also specify whether any tangible personal property located on the real property is included in the bequest.

If you want a beneficiary to inherit a specific item of property free of any debt, then language in the Will must specifically state this. It is also good practice to specify that the property is distributed subject to encumbrances if that is the case (for example, in the case of real property, "subject to all encumbrances, including, but not limited to mortgages, deeds of trust, and real property taxes and assessments"). This eliminates any ambiguity and minimizes the potential for dispute.

If you want property to be distributed free and clear, then, generally, the residue of the estate will bear the expense of satisfying the debt, unless the Will specifies another payment source. Consider how the application of these rules could affect the inheritance received by other beneficiaries, particularly residuary beneficiaries.

TANGIBLE PERSONAL PROPERTY

Tangible personal property is generally understood to be property that can be seen, weighed, and measured; has a location; and can be possessed and touched. It includes items such as furniture, automobiles, boats, pets, and jewelry.

Generally you either select specific items to give to specific individuals, give all tangible personal property to one person or a group of people, or give the Executor discretion to divide it as they see fit.

Spouses will often give all of their tangible personal property to one another. A surviving parent may give all tangible personal property to the children, to be divided as they agree.

Give careful consideration to the division and distribution of these items, as they often have sentimental value that may trigger family disputes regardless of the property's monetary value.

Some may benefit from cataloguing valuable tangible personal property, such as artwork and jewelry, by photograph and with a detailed description.

Asset Catalog: Debra's brother, Alfred D. Kleyhauer III, was an artist who pre-deceased her. Part of her estate planning identifies specific paintings to be donated to a collection upon her death. A color anthology with images of all his artwork was used to identify specific gifts for clarity.

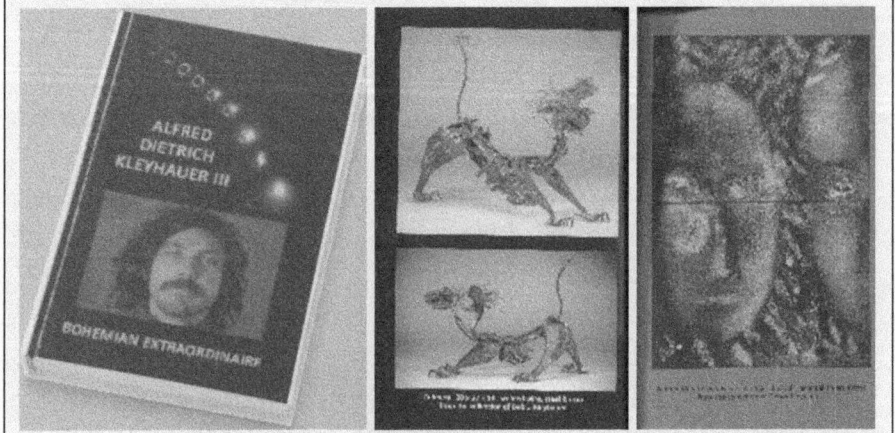

GIFTS BY MEMORANDUM

In Pennsylvania, it is common practice to include an option in a Will to distribute personal property by a separate memorandum or "side list." It can be used to designate significant personal property.

If naming and designating such gifts is likely to take so long that it prevents the timely completion of a Will, it can be very elegant to use such a side list. Also, the side list is easier to update than a Will, as frequently, older people begin to give away possessions while they are still alive.

One interesting aspect of designating gifts in a side list is that this document is not presented to the Register of Wills – which means it's not seen by any government official.

In contrast, if an item is part of the Will itself, then it becomes a matter of public record. Additionally, the Executor may need to obtain an appraisal for the item, which comes at a cost.

Another benefit of the side list is that if assets are referenced in the Will but have been given away before death, no one has to justify what happened to them.

To be legally enforceable, this memorandum, or side list, must either satisfy the common law incorporation by reference doctrine, or qualify as a Codicil to the Will which would be entitled to probate – meaning that it must be executed with all of the same formalities as a Will.

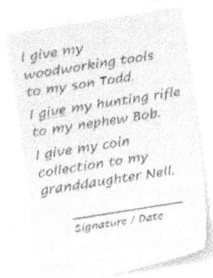

I give my woodworking tools to my son Todd.
I give my hunting rifle to my nephew Bob.
I give my coin collection to my granddaughter Nell.

Signature / Date

Even if the memorandum is not legally binding, it can serve as a valuable tool for the Executor, clarifying how to divide personal property among beneficiaries. It can also help prevent hard feelings among family members.

The most common way for the side list to be made legally enforceable is for it to be handwritten and signed.

Its terms should not conflict with the Will. Although not required by law, it is helpful for all outside memoranda to be dated in case subsequent ones contain conflicting provisions.

In some circumstances, an outside memorandum *should not* be used. For example:

- If you are unlikely to communicate with counsel or the Executor regarding the status of an outside memorandum and where to find it, it is often better to include all provisions in the Will.

- If there is any concern that you may be incompetent or susceptible to undue influence, an outside memorandum may not be suitable, as there will likely be no attorney oversight to ensure its validity.

- If there is a concern that a beneficiary omitted from the memorandum may have an incentive to destroy it following your death.

- For extremely valuable items, one should consider writing the gifts into the Will itself. Separate lists of personal property items are generally more suitable for miscellaneous household goods and items of nominal value.

The memorandum should be kept with other estate planning documents, and ideally, an executed original should also be maintained on file by trusted counsel.

RESIDUARY GIFTS

A "residuary bequest" gifts whatever remains of your estate after payment of debts, costs of administration, funeral expenses, and specific and general bequests. Depending on the estate plan, the residuary bequest can be the smallest or the largest disposition in the Will.

Even if you intend to give all known estate assets through specific gift clauses in the Will, the Will should always include a residuary clause because it's difficult to predict, between the time the Will is made and the time of death, if you will own assets that were not specifically gifted, if a gift will be disclaimed, or if a named beneficiary will die first.

ULTIMATE CONTINGENCY CLAUSE – "GIFT-OVER"

Most Wills also include an ultimate contingency clause in case of catastrophe where many of the heirs die at the same time. This clause usually directs the residuary property to relatives entitled to inherit under the intestate succession statute, or to charities. However, you can include any contingent beneficiaries that you desire.

In the absence of this provision, intestacy laws apply to any property not otherwise effectively disposed of. Beware, as relying on intestacy laws alone can lead to unanticipated results.

UPDATING A WILL

Decades ago, Wills were prepared on a typewriter. Before that they were handwritten. Because substantial effort would be required to re-do the document, an update could be prepared, called a *Codicil*. This had the same execution requirements and formality.

These days, thanks to computers, it's very simple to change designations within a Will. However, if an amendment is small, it may still be easier to do through a Codicil. It all depends on how long it's been and what issues have come into play.

TRUSTS

We'll cover Trusts in detail in Chapter Six, but for now you should understand that a Trust is a fund set up for a specific planning purpose. Although creating and funding a Trust is more work up front, Trusts can save substantial time and money after the Testator's death by:

- Avoiding the need for a court-appointed Guardian in the event of your incapacity

- Avoiding or minimizing probate

- Providing a private realm for distributing property

Trusts can also be established for the benefit of an individual like a spouse or minor children.

WHEN

There are a few checkpoints in life when people give serious consideration to drafting a Will:

- Marriage
- Birth of a child
- When a child turns 18
- Significant travel
- Birth of a grandchild
- Medical diagnosis or surgery
- Divorce

In addition to the above-mentioned predictable life events, it is not uncommon for people to feel the need to create a Will after learning of the unexpected death of a friend, loved one, or even a celebrity.

WHY

A Will controls assets that are owned by a person at the time of death and that do not pass by survivorship or beneficiary designation.

Assets that pass under the Will are called *probate assets*. In addition to typical items, these can include refunds issued after date of death – such as income tax refunds, overpayments of insurance and other premiums, utility account refunds, and overpayments of monthly rent at assisted living facilities and nursing homes. For this reason, even if you use a Trust as the primary estate planning vehicle, you should have a pour-over Will to provide for assets not transferred to the Trust during your lifetime.

A Will may not control all assets, however. For example, property that is held in a revocable or irrevocable Trust, property that is held jointly with a right of survivorship, and property that has a beneficiary designation do not pass by Will. Because of this, you may view a Will as unnecessary, particularly if all of the assets are held in a way that allows them to pass without the need for a Will.

Whether the Will is your primary estate planning vehicle or a back-up to a revocable Trust, you should consider the role of *non-probate assets*. These include assets and contractual benefits – such as bank accounts, brokerage accounts, certificates of deposit, life insurance policies, retirement accounts, and real estate. These assets name a designated beneficiary within them. It is imperative to coordinate such non-probate assets with probate assets for an effective estate plan, so you understand how each asset will pass (and to whom).

Failure to consider and verify ownership and beneficiary designations may undermine the estate plan, which could lead to additional taxes, family conflict, litigation, and claims.

Improper titling of assets may undermine estate plans... and increase expense.

If there is a conflict between a Will provision and a beneficiary designation or survivorship right, the beneficiary designation or survivorship right controls. For example, if you leave real estate to a beneficiary in a Will, but the property was owned in a joint tenancy with right of survivorship, the title controls and the property passes to the surviving joint tenant, not to the beneficiary designated in the Will.

Pay-on-death and transfer-on-death accounts also need to be coordinated with the estate plan, as beneficiaries named on those accounts receive the accounts regardless of any provision in a Will. Retirement accounts that list a beneficiary will also be distributed to the designated beneficiary, even if the Will specifies otherwise.

Titling assets correctly is especially important if the success of the estate plan depends on it. For example, if an insurance policy is purchased for the express purpose of providing liquidity to pay anticipated estate taxes, but the named beneficiary on the life insurance policy is an individual rather than the estate, then the estate would not have access to those funds and therefore may not be able to pay the taxes.

Another potential pitfall is if all assets are titled in the name of one spouse, but the other spouse dies first. To avoid this, assets should be titled jointly during the planning phase.

Such failure to properly designate beneficiaries or ensure that assets are properly titled can also result in unnecessary probate fees and vulnerability to creditors. This can happen if, instead of passing to an intended beneficiary, non-probate property unintentionally becomes part of a probate estate.

In simple estates, like the case of a husband and wife, probate is often unnecessary. All or most of the property can be transferred outside of the probate process. The most common planning techniques are the use of:

- Joint titling, beneficiary designations, or both as the primary vehicles for transfer

- A revocable Trust

- Life estates as part of the transfer plan

If you die without a Will, but while owning assets that do not otherwise pass by title or beneficiary designation, those assets will pass by intestacy, which we'll talk about later.

JOINT OWNERSHIP AND BENEFICIARY DESIGNATIONS

Some may want to rely solely on rights of survivorship and beneficiary designations to transfer assets. This can work in certain circumstances, such as when spouses hold all or most of their assets jointly and have named each other as beneficiary on all retirement accounts and insurance policies.

However, in more complex estates, Wills are good tools for addressing matters that may be overlooked or that cannot be accomplished solely by joint titling and beneficiary designation.

Wills are particularly advantageous when there are:

- Minor beneficiaries

- Beneficiaries with special needs

- Elderly beneficiaries

- Multiple beneficiaries, especially if some do not get along well

- Beneficiaries with creditor or marital problems

- Beneficiaries with personal issues, such as addiction

- Many specific gifts

- Complex formulas for allocation of gifts

- Gifts to be distributed over time

- Gifts to be distributed on the occurrence of specific events

- Complex contingencies for failed gifts

- Gifts with no title or beneficiary designation, such as artwork, jewelry, valuable collections, and photographs

- Concerns about inheritance tax planning

Even in simple estates where joint tenancy and beneficiary designations are appropriate substitutes, there should still be a Will to function as a backup plan or catch-all provision if unforeseen circumstances should arise. Failure to include a Will in planning that relies primarily on joint titling and beneficiary designations can result in distributions that don't align with the deceased's wishes if those designations fail.

LIFE ESTATES

A life estate allows an owner of real property to both retain an interest in the real property during their lifetime, and leave the remainder interest in the property to one or more designated beneficiaries upon their death.

This type of ownership avoids probate because the property interest is vested in the remaindermen at the time the life estate is created.

The owner of real property creates a life estate by executing a quit claim deed retaining a life estate, and designating one or more remainder beneficiaries.

On the owner's death, the life estate terminates and the remainder interest passes to the designated beneficiaries. To reflect the new ownership in the public records, counsel or the new owners should record the death certificate of the life estate holder.

One disadvantage to a traditional life estate, however, is that the life tenant owes a duty to the remainder beneficiaries and cannot diminish or alter the value of that person's future estate.

IN THE CASE OF DIVORCE

There are provisions of state law that dictate what a divorce will or won't do to prior beneficiary designations. Things like a 401K rise under federal law though. It's important to remember that the terms of the divorce take effect on the date of the decree, not a separation.

It's not uncommon for divorced people to fail to follow up on beneficiary designations. They could die, believing everything would be inherited by the children or a new partner, but if the Will or a life insurance or 401K fund still has the previous spouse designated as the beneficiary, that former spouse receives the benefits.

As with all major life changes, a divorce is something that should definitely prompt you to review, and presumably update, estate planning.

DISINHERITANCE

If a person is not specifically provided for in a Will, that person generally does not inherit under the Will. However, two notable exceptions may apply in the case of spouses and children, including children born or adopted after a Will has been executed.

Sometimes a person's Will does not specifically name an heir as beneficiary but also does not specifically exclude that heir. In this case, it is possible that the heir will inherit anyway.

Disinheriting a Spouse
In Pennsylvania, spouses cannot disinherit each other completely unless there is a valid prenuptial or post-nuptial agreement whereby a spouse waives the right to inherit and to claim an elective share. Absent this waiver, there are two remedies.

If you signed the Will while married to a surviving spouse, the elective share is available for the surviving spouse whether or not the spouse is provided for in your Will. The elective share is a statutory amount equal to one-third of the decedent's augmented estate. The augmented estate includes the probate estate as well as interests in other, non-probate assets.

Certain property is specifically excluded from the elective share unless it passes through the decedent's estate:

- Any conveyance made with the express consent or joinder of the surviving spouse

- Proceeds of insurance, including accidental death benefits, on the life of the decedent

- Interests under any broad-based nondiscriminatory pension, profit sharing, stock bonus, deferred compensation, disability, death benefit, or other such plan established by an employer for the benefit of its employees and their beneficiaries

- Property passing by the decedent's exercise or non-exercise of any power of appointment given by someone other than the decedent

If you signed the Will before marrying a surviving spouse, that spouse may be eligible to take either a pretermitted spouse's share or an elective share.

A surviving spouse is entitled to a pretermitted spouse's share unless:

- The Will gives the surviving spouse a greater share

- It appears from the Will that the Will was made in contemplation of marriage to the surviving spouse

The pretermitted spouse's share is equal to a spouse's intestate share, which can range from one-half of the intestate estate to all of the intestate estate, depending on whether the decedent has living parents or issue.

A disinherited spouse must consider both the elective share and the pretermitted share and determine which is most beneficial, if both apply. Although the pretermitted spouse's share entitles a surviving spouse to a larger percentage of the assets, it may apply to a much smaller pool of assets.

Disinheriting a Child
A child generally has no right under Pennsylvania law to inherit from a parent, subject to a few exceptions. A child born before you sign a Will who is not included in that Will is entitled to a family exemption if:

- You had no surviving spouse

- The child was a member of your household at the time of your death

If a child is born or adopted after a parent's Will is signed, and is not provided for in the Will, that child is treated as a *pretermitted* child, unless it appears in the Will that the omission was intentional. If a child is treated as a pretermitted child:

- The child inherits from the Testator parent.

- The child receives the share the child would have received if the deceased parent had died unmarried and intestate.

- The pretermitted child share is paid from the Testator's property that does not pass to the surviving spouse.

Inadvertent Inheritance
If you wish to disinherit adult children or other heirs, the Will should expressly disinherit those individuals to ensure they do not inadvertently take if:

- All named beneficiaries predecease

- All named beneficiaries disclaim

- The Will uses class language to describe beneficiaries (for example, "my heirs")

If all named beneficiaries die first or disclaim, the Will may default to intestacy and inadvertently include a person intended to be disinherited. If the Will uses class language, the person to be disinherited may inadvertently inherit if not expressly excluded from the definition of heirs (for example, "to my heirs, not including my brother Jacob Smith, or his issue").

Be mindful of your beneficiaries who are recognized by law, including your spouse and children. If you desire to disinherit one or more of them, you should be deliberate and mindful of rights that might exist to those beneficiaries under applicable law. Once again, deliberate planning is the means to achieve specific results. If your estate plan defaults to the applicable provisions of the law, it may not implement your wishes.

No-Contest Clauses
Another common way to disinherit beneficiaries is by using a no-contest clause (sometimes referred to as a penalty clause). This is designed to prevent someone from contesting provisions of a Will or Trust.

No-contest clauses are valid in Pennsylvania, but are unenforceable when probable cause exists for instituting proceedings.

Unless a potential contestant actually receives a significant bequest under the Will or Trust, the contestant does not stand to lose anything significant by contesting. If you are sincerely worried about a party contesting the Will, you must provide a bequest significant enough that the beneficiary would consider not contesting the Will for fear of losing the bequest.

GROUNDS FOR INVALIDITY OF WILL

A Will or Codicil can be challenged if there is a lack of compliance with formalities, it has been revoked by you, you lacked testamentary capacity, or if there was undue influence, fraud, duress, coercion, or mistake.

INTESTACY

If the Will fails, beneficiaries predecease, or assets are not validly disposed by the Will, revocable Trust, joint tenancy, beneficiary designation, or otherwise, the Commonwealth of Pennsylvania provides for the assets to be distributed according to the statutes governing intestate succession.

When assets pass by intestacy, the Commonwealth of Pennsylvania determines who receives the deceased's property, in what order, and in what shares.

If no heirs under the statute can be located, the property will revert to the state. Under intestacy rules, the Commonwealth of Pennsylvania is not the default beneficiary unless *all* of the other prescribed beneficiaries predecease the decedent.

For this reason, it is valuable to have a Will in place, and to consider having multiple layers of named beneficiaries, so that in the event of catastrophe like a house fire or plane crash affecting multiple family members, your wishes can still be honored.

When a resident of the Commonwealth of Pennsylvania dies without a Will, assets pass by order of intestacy, as noted below:

1. Surviving spouse

2. Children and grandchildren

3. Surviving parents

4. Surviving siblings and their children

5. Surviving grandparents

6. Surviving uncles and aunts

7. Surviving nieces and nephews

8. The Commonwealth, in the event no other surviving heirs can be located

Many people complete estate planning to specifically avoid the possibility of their property going to the government. As you can see from the list above, the government could become your inadvertent beneficiary if you fail to take action to avoid it.

HOW TO CREATE A LAST WILL AND TESTAMENT

To be valid under Pennsylvania law, a Will must be:

- Executed by an individual 18 years of age or older who is of sound mind

- In writing

- Signed or marked by you, or signed by another person in your presence of, or at your direction

If you are physically capable of signing the Will, this should be done, even if your signature is shaky. If, as a result, your signature looks different from prior signatures, it should be documented, which may help if your signature is later challenged.

In the event the Will is signed by your mark or by another person at your request, it should be signed in the presence of two or more credible witnesses, each of whom signs in your presence.

Allegations of fraud regarding signatures can be minimized through notations on the various pages of the Will, and placing an executed copy in safekeeping. No one should write on the Will, alter it, remove staples, or take apart bound pages.

WITNESSES

While Pennsylvania law does not require your signature to be witnessed, in order for it to be admitted to probate, it must be proved by the oath or affirmation of two competent witnesses. Accordingly, it is best practice to have two disinterested and competent witnesses[6] sign a "self-proving affidavit" to ease probate.

A Will that is self-proved is admitted to probate without having to submit additional proof that it was executed in conformity with Pennsylvania law. A self-proving affidavit is usually made a part of a Will, as an attachment at the end, but it can be signed after the Will's execution. The self-proving affidavit must be accepted by the Register of Wills as proof of the facts stated as if the affidavit had been made under oath before the Register at the time of probate.

The self-proving affidavit consists of two parts: the acknowledgment signed by you, and the affidavits signed by the witnesses, all of which are notarized.

In the acknowledgment, you swear the document was voluntarily signed and executed. In the affidavit, the witnesses swear: that you signed and executed the document as a Will, voluntarily and in front of the witnesses; that the witnesses each signed in your presence; and to the best of the witness's knowledge, you were over age 18 and of sound mind and not under constraint or undue influence at the time the Will was signed.

A notary then acknowledges your and witnesses' statements and identities. Alternatively, the self-proving affidavit may be executed in the presence of an attorney licensed to practice in the state of execution. The attorney must then sign an

---

[6] Be sure to document and retain up-to-date address, email, and phone number for these witnesses in case they need to be contacted in the future.

additional acknowledgment in front of a notary or other person authorized to administer oaths.

A self-proving affidavit is not required to make a valid Will, but it can save valuable time during the probate process. If the self-proving affidavit is not submitted with the Will, the petitioner will have to gather proof that the Will was properly executed, which can be troublesome if witnesses cannot be located or if they have died. All estate planning should include a self-proving affidavit as part of every Will execution, if practicable.

OUT-OF-STATE, HOLOGRAPHIC, AND NUNCUPATIVE WILLS

Certain types of wills may be treated differently under Pennsylvania law. These include:

- Wills that were signed by a person who was not a resident of Pennsylvania at the time the Will was signed

- Handwritten wills

- Oral wills

- Contractual wills

Let's look at these one at a time.

Out-of-State Wills

Pennsylvania gives full faith and credit to the laws of other states regarding the execution of Wills within their jurisdiction that are later submitted to probate in Pennsylvania. Except for nuncupative wills (see below), a Will executed in conformity with another state's or country's requirements is considered valid in Pennsylvania if it is valid under the laws of the state or country where it was executed... even if it does not comply with Pennsylvania's requirements.

Handwritten Wills

A "holographic" Will is generally understood to be a handwritten Will that is signed but not witnessed. Because

Pennsylvania does not require Wills to be witnessed, holographic Wills are valid in Pennsylvania.

Oral Wills

A nuncupative Will is an oral or unwritten Will. Nuncupative Wills are *not* valid in Pennsylvania. The classic nuncupative Will is one in which you make a deathbed oral declaration to relatives.

Contractual Wills

In Pennsylvania, a person can enter into a binding agreement or contract concerning the succession of their estate. A person may agree to:

- Die without a Will

- Make a Will or testamentary provision

- Not revoke an existing Will or testamentary provision

- Make the estate bound by an obligation dischargeable only at or after the person's death.

After your death, the agreement can only be established by one or more of the following:

- A provision in the Will stating the material provisions of the contract

- An express reference in the Will to the contract and extrinsic evidence proving the contract's terms

- A signed writing evidencing the contract

There is no presumption that you and your spouse entered into a contract to make a Will or not revoke a Will just because you executed joint or mutual Wills.

IDENTIFYING HEIRS

Most people want to leave gifts to children and grandchildren in their Will or Trust. Such plans often raise a few questions, which can be addressed with prudent planning. Specifically, must each child or grandchild be named? And what if more are born after the Will or Trust is executed?

If planning documents are well written, they can both manage your wishes and handle certain, foreseeable family changes.

The solution is to identify such beneficiaries as part of a class. The law considers your "issue" to be your lineal descendants (those individuals who follow you in your bloodline) or offspring. So, a gift could be left to "my issue," which would include all children living at the time of your death, even if they were born after the Will was signed. Similarly, you could make a gift to "all grandchildren" who are living at the time of your death.

MODIFYING OR REVOKING A WILL

You may change a Will either by executing a new Will, modifying an existing Will by Codicil, or revoking a Will in its entirety.

A Codicil amends an existing Will by adding, altering, substituting, or deleting any part of a Will, and must be executed in the same manner as a Will to be valid. The Will and all Codicils are considered a single instrument and are read together.

A Will may be modified by law based on certain changes in your circumstances, including divorce or pending divorce, marriage, birth or adoption of a child, or to preclude any person who participated in your willful and unlawful killing.

Using a Codicil to make modifications to a Will provides a paper trail of your changing wishes. In a probate proceeding, both the

Will and Codicil are available for inspection by anyone once filed because probate records are public.

If you reduce a beneficiary's share by Codicil, the beneficiary would have access, as part of the routine probate process, to the original Will and the Codicil that reduced their share. If, on the other hand, you execute an entirely new Will that either reduces a beneficiary's share or omits the beneficiary entirely, that beneficiary would not have access to the prior Will as part of the routine probate process and would not necessarily be aware of the reduction or elimination of his interest. In any of these circumstances, it is often easier and more beneficial to prepare a new Will.

You may revoke a Will by:

- Executing a later Will declaring the revocation

- Executing a later Will to the extent that it is inconsistent with the prior Will

- Intentionally burning, canceling, tearing, obliterating, or destroying it with the intent and purpose of revocation. This can also be done by another person:

    o in your presence;
    o at your direction; and
    o with your direction proven by two competent witnesses.

A revoked Will cannot be revived except by re-execution of the Will or an instrument stating your intent to revive the earlier Will.

EFFECT OF SUBSEQUENT EVENTS ON WILL

Certain life events that take place after a Will is executed could change the terms of the Will, including marriage, birth, adoption, divorce, and annulment.

If you get married, have a child, or adopt a child after executing a Will and the Will does not contemplate that event happening, the pretermitted spouse or child may receive a share of the estate.

If you marry after making a Will, the surviving spouse receives the share that would be received had you died intestate, unless:

- The Will gave a greater share

- It appears from the Will that it was made in contemplation of the marriage

If you have or adopt a child after executing a Will in which provisions are not made for the child, unless it appears from the Will that the omission was intentional, the child will receive the share that would have been received had you died unmarried, intestate, or owning only the portion of the estate not passing to the surviving spouse. The share is paid out of property not passing to the surviving spouse.

Unless a Will provides otherwise, all provisions that affect a former spouse become ineffective if you are divorced from the spouse after making the Will, or die domiciled in Pennsylvania during divorce proceedings after grounds have been established.

NOMINATING A GUARDIAN

For a parent with minor children, the most important issue in the estate plan is usually naming the person who will act as Guardian of your children.

Guardianship provisions are not likely to be needed unless both parents die while the child is still a minor. However, they should be included in the unlikely event that both parents die simultaneously or too close in time for the surviving parent to update their own Will.

Guardianship gives legal custody of a minor child, the minor's estate (that is, the minor's assets), or both, to the appointed Guardian.

At the time a named Guardian petitions the court for guardianship, the Guardian *must not* be:

- Under 18 years of age

- A corporation not authorized to act as fiduciary in Pennsylvania

- A parent of the minor, except if the parent is appointed Co-Guardian with another

When nominating a Guardian, consider whether that person is capable of accepting custody and caring for the child in an acceptable manner, should it be necessary. Ideally it should be someone you are close to and whom you trust to make good decisions, and with whom the minor children will be most comfortable.

Naming a Guardian in a Will does not guarantee that person will be appointed. If another party challenges the appointment, however, that outside party bears the burden of producing clear and convincing evidence that the named Guardian is not in the best interest of the child. Thus, naming a Guardian in the Will makes it more likely that the desired person will be appointed.

A divorced or single parent *may* nominate a Guardian, but such a decision may not be legally binding if the other parent is still living (absent a termination of parental rights). Instead, they may appoint a Guardian of the estate for the property passing to the child.

A Guardian of the estate of a minor child is necessary if the minor child receives funds outright (as opposed to in a Trust). This can happen in several ways, including:

- Under the parent's Will

- From sources other than the parent
- By beneficiary designation

When possible, it is best to select a single individual to act as Guardian of a minor's person and property. However, if you feel a certain individual should have custody of a minor child but do not believe that person is capable of handling the minor's finances, this is an option.

Preparing a comprehensive Power of Attorney may make guardianship proceedings unnecessary, and is much less expensive and stressful than court proceedings.

Bryan Tate
York County
Register of Wills & Clerk of Orphans Court

"The Orphans Court is in charge of proceedings including dockets and filings for petitions of incapacitated persons, for the appointment of Guardians, for the termination of parental rights, as well as adoptions. There are two types of guardianship: guardianship of the body and guardianship of the estate. There's often confusion between 'custody' and 'guardianship.' *Custody* is typically between parents as part of a divorce settlement, while *guardianship* is for overseeing either the financial aspects of somebody's life who is important to them, or their health and wellbeing.

The process begins with a nine-page questionnaire, typically completed by an attorney. It asks questions about the individual who is petitioning for guardianship and about the person who is to be deemed incapacitated. It's really how the judge and the court starts its decision-making process. The process could take a month or a couple of months. It really depends on how prepared individuals are. That's why I encourage folks to seek legal representation. That professional will make sure you are best prepared."

NOMINATING A CUSTODIAN

If you do not want to name a Guardian or create a Trust for minor children, but still want to protect assets that may pass to minor children, a Custodian can be named under the Pennsylvania Uniform Transfers to Minors Act.

A Will may nominate a Custodian to hold the minor's property or can empower the Executor or Administrator to transfer property to a person: "as Custodian for [MINOR NAME] under the Pennsylvania Uniform Transfers to Minors Act." Only one Custodian may serve at a time, but a Will can name successor Custodians.

If the Will fails to nominate a Custodian, the Executor or Administrator may designate one. A child who is at least 14 years of age may also designate a successor Custodian for himself or herself.

Types of custodial property include, but are not limited to, real property, tangible personal property, securities, money, life insurance policies, annuities, powers of appointment, contractual rights, and certificates of title.

The nomination of a Custodian does not create custodial property until an irrevocable transfer of the property to the nominated Custodian is completed. A custodianship can be conditioned on the occurrence of a future event, typically your death. Unless revoked, on the occurrence of the future event, the custodianship becomes effective and the Custodian can enforce the transfer of custodial property.

A Custodian is generally held to the prudent person standard in managing custodial property. With that limitation, the Custodian has all of the rights, powers, and authority over custodial property that unmarried adult owners have over their own property, which the Custodian may only exercise in that custodial capacity.

The Custodian may use the custodial property for the minor's benefit without court order, considering if other property is available to the minor, or if others are personally responsible for supporting the minor.

The custodianship terminates when the minor reaches age 21, unless the transferor has specified a later time for transfer (up to age 25).

Added Benefits of Having Counsel
In addition to the peace of mind offered by having professional guidance when creating your Last Will and Testament, trusted counsel will also usually store that executed original Will in case any unforeseen needs arise.

For example, my office creates one original of this document:

I hold this original executed Will, free of charge to the client. However, I provide copies of the Will with an obvious notation on the front page that the original is in safe storage at the firm.

Keeping the original Will in a known safe place decreases the likelihood it might get lost. It also prevents an individual, who is often older, from hand marking changes to the original Will. Such handwritten changes create all sorts of complications as to whether or not the changes are in fact valid. It can definitely create disharmony in the family.

My grandmother, Elle, in her older years, thought about making many changes to her Will. She was a Notary so she thought she could create her own documents to do so. Fortunately, I was able to help her implement changes to her Will – appropriately, properly, and effectively.

CAUTIONARY TALES

1 Don't store your Will in a safe deposit box. Once a person dies, the only way for someone else to gain access to the safe deposit box is to have Letters of Administration – meaning they've been named Administrator of the estate. But the only way for this to happen is for the Will to be submitted to the court. And if they don't have the Will already, and they can't get access to it in the safe deposit box, for all effective purposes, the Will does not exist.

2 Let someone know where your important documents are stored. This can be accomplished through a conversation, or through the Final Instruction Letter we'll talk about in Chapter Seven.

Your up-to-date estate plan only works when the people who are responsible for carrying it out know where it is. When Olympic medalist Florence Griffith Joyner died at age 38, her family couldn't locate her Will. This led to disputes between her husband and mother which could have easily been avoided.

3 Get help from trusted counsel. When James Gandolfini of *Sopranos* fame died in 2013, even though he had a Will which provided for his family, the estate plan didn't have proper tax planning. As a result, his $70M estate ended up paying federal and state estate taxes at a rate of 55 percent – which could have been significantly reduced or eliminated altogether with proper planning.

4 Don't fail to preserve a life estate. It's not uncommon with second marriages for the couple to move into one of their two homes, which remains in only the original owner's name. Even if the owning spouse wants his or her biological children to inherit the home, the Will can designate that the remaining spouse be allowed to live in the house as long as desired, paying the taxes and maintenance and insurance while residing there.

5 There are situations where inheritance creates a tax burden and there are not enough liquid assets to cover. One of the provisions in a Will is typically a tax provision stating either the estate will pay taxes on anything that's inherited or the recipient will pay the taxes. If it's a non-probate asset, the recipient will often get billed. If you're on a bank account as a joint owner and the other person dies, mandated reporting from the bank triggers the state to send you a bill for the inheritance tax from the other half.

Example: Three siblings inherit the family home. The daughter wants to keep it but the sons want to sell. There's no money to pay the taxes and other probate fees. Someone has to put up money to clear the estate because if taxes aren't addressed – especially real estate – potentially they could lose it all.

6 Don't let perfect be the enemy of good. Essentially, don't wait for some "perfect time" to create your Will. When pop singer Prince died at age 57 without a Will, his $150M estate was left to be dealt with by Minnesota state law, and as such, was open and available for public scrutiny.

Just remember, you don't need to have millions of dollars in the bank or under your mattress for a Will to make a difference in the future lives of your loved ones. A little bit of planning today can save them additional heartache and frustration at a time when they will already be grieving. What better way to feel confident that your family will be taken care of, no matter what?

MAKE DOCUMENTS
ACCESSIBLE

SET GOALS

ABSOLVE FAMILY
OF BURDEN

S.M.A.R.T.

TAKE CARE OF
LOVED ONES

RELIEVE

CHAOS

&

CONFUSION

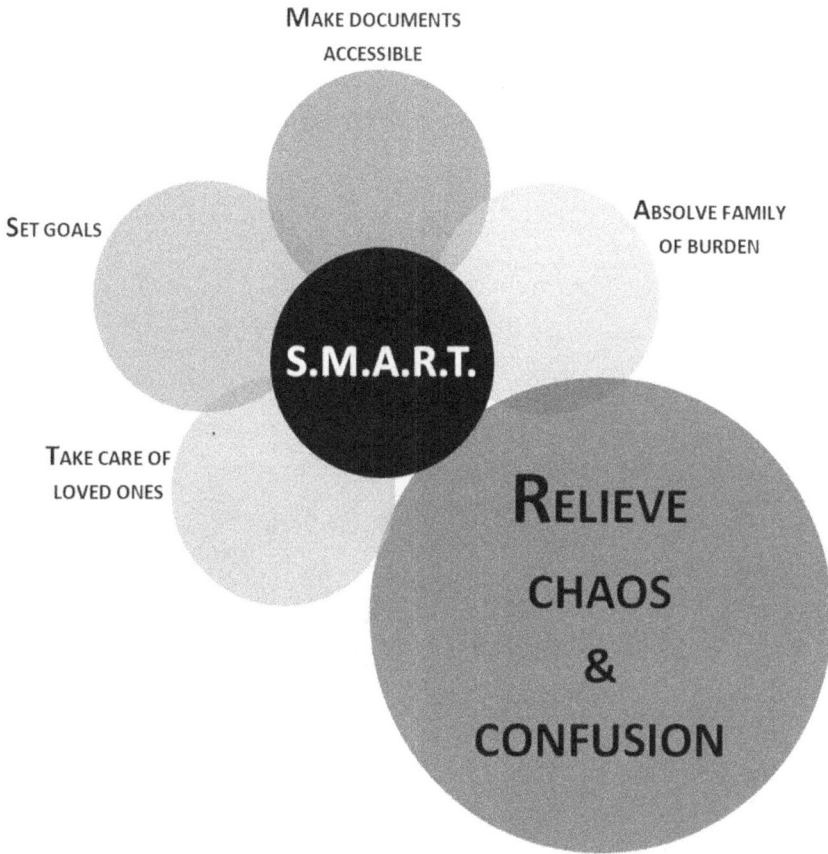

How can you **RELIEVE CHAOS & CONFUSION** that surrounds the death of a loved one?

☐ Consider who to select as **Executor/Executrix** for the estate.

☐ Consider who to select if a **Guardian** might be necessary for minor children or pets.

☐ Consider who to name as **Trustee** for any funds placed in Trust to benefit your loved ones or charity.

□ Make an appointment with trusted counsel to begin preparing the **Last Will & Testament.**

□ Complete the **Estate Planning Questionnaire** document in Appendix B (page 211).

For downloadable forms, visit

www.SMARTestateplanbook.com

Schedule an Appointment

(717) 848-4900 (office)
(717) 718-7115 (direct)
jrehmeyer@cgalaw.com

6 TRUSTS

A Trust is a fund set up with specific goals or purposes to achieve. It is a legal entity, established by a document, that can include assets like real estate, bank accounts, investments, and tangible property (such as equipment, supplies, jewelry, or fine art). The Trust then serves as a mechanism to preserve wealth and utilize it for yourself or your loved ones.

Trusts can help you:

- Avoid the need for a court-appointed Guardian in the event of your incapacity

- Avoid or minimize probate

- Provide a private realm for distributing property

Trusts can also be established for the benefit of an individual like a spouse or minor children.

For all Wills that involve minor children, I recommend a Trust which designates a Trustee (an individual or entity who will make decisions on behalf of your wishes or the best interests of minor children). Trust funds can typically be used toward the maintenance, education, and health needs of the beneficiaries as required.

You can also support individuals with special needs or certain disabilities, and Trusts can be written with specific language so they don't interfere with government aid.

Remember that a Trust, just like a Will, can be updated over time. As situations change, language can be altered to best express your current wishes. For example, if a family rift has healed, you might wish a previously excluded sibling or child or spouse to now receive allocations from your Trust.

Let's take a more detailed look at the *Who, What, When, Why* and *How* of Trusts.

WHO

The **Settlor** is the person creating the Trust.

The **Trustee** is the individual(s) or an institution who administers the instructions of the Trust.

The **Beneficiary** is a person, institution, or even a pet that receives benefits from the assets of the Trust. There may be one or more named beneficiaries, and allocations can vary. For example, Trust distributions could include an outright gift of property, an annual income generated from Trust assets, or discretionary gifts to provide for someone who cannot handle the allocations themselves, such as a minor child.

CHOOSING A TRUSTEE

During your lifetime, you may choose to serve as the primary Trustee, managing assets of the Trust yourself. Whoever you choose for the role should be someone you are confident will carry out your wishes and protect your beneficiaries.

Trustees are responsible for administering a Trust in accordance with your wishes and for the benefit of its beneficiaries. The Trustee may also collect assets, such as proceeds from life insurance policies, when the Trust is named directly as beneficiary.

A Trust can also have multiple Trustees, who can either all serve in the same capacity or may have distinct duties.

Depending on your choice of Trustee(s), you may want to pay them for their time or reimburse them in some way for their service. If you have chosen to use a corporate fiduciary to manage your Trust, you will most definitely need to consider what kind of compensation will be required.

When large or complex Trusts are created, you should consider either nominating a corporate Trustee or granting someone the power under the Will to nominate a corporate Trustee if it becomes necessary.

Corporate Trustees are typically bank trust departments or independent trust companies. The advantage of a corporate Trustee is that it has the experience and expertise required to deal with both Trust investments and beneficiaries. A corporate Trustee is a neutral third-party, though this person may not be familiar with family dynamics and will typically charge higher fees than an individual Trustee.

Regardless of what type of Trustee is nominated, this person should be trustworthy, have financial capability, and have no potential conflicts of interest with the beneficiaries.

Trustees must administer the Trust in good faith and are generally held to the prudent investor rule, however the Trust instrument may alter or eliminate the prudent investor rule and provide its own standards for managing and investing Trust assets that will override the statutory standard.

> Susan's mother was in need of updated estate planning, which had last been addressed when her father died some years ago. Susan had served as Trustee under a Trust for a number of years. During the conversation, it became apparent that she didn't fully understand the benefits of the Trust, nor did she enjoy serving as Trustee, even though she presumed it was beneficial for her mother and therefore her family.

Just as you should be aware of the benefits of a Trust, and confirm that they will help you achieve your desired goals, similarly, that knowledge should be passed on to your Trustee and others named in the Trust. Estate planning documents such as a Will can sometimes be lengthy. However, Trusts are typically the longest of all estate planning documents. Therefore, the act of understanding them and appreciating their significance is even more challenging. So, make sure that you (or your attorney) speaks with your Trustee too.

WHAT

A Trust may either by *revocable* or *irrevocable*. Revocable Trusts can be set up and undone if needed. They are commonly created to allocate assets while you are living. You can place assets in such a Trust but still do whatever you want with them. The opposite is true of an irrevocable Trust. Once assets are designated to an irrevocable Trust, they cannot be removed.

Revocable Trusts and Pour-over Wills

The key purposes of planning with a revocable Trust are to avoid or minimize probate, and to avoid a guardianship proceeding if you become incapacitated. Sometimes a revocable Trust is called a "Living Trust," and many times they are proposed as a substitute for a Will, in order to avoid probate.

This plan works well when the Trust is properly funded and appropriate beneficiary designations are in place. It takes both extensive documentation and attention to detail. The benefits of a revocable Trust are only realized if it's been properly implemented. Otherwise, you might simply spend too much money without realizing the results you were seeking.

Whenever a revocable Trust is used as the primary estate planning vehicle, it should be accompanied by a pour-over Will that distributes the residue of the estate directly to the revocable Trust. This residuary clause will capture all property that was not transferred to the Trust before your death.

Unfortunately, people with revocable Trusts in place often still die with assets that must pass through the probate process. This can happen for many reasons, including that you:

- Forget you own an asset in your individual name

- Mistakenly believe the Trust was already funded with a particular asset

- Fail to revise beneficiary designations to name the Trust as beneficiary, potentially causing the underlying asset to become directly payable to someone without the benefit of the protections of the Trust

- Neglect to update ownership on all existing bank and securities accounts

- Forget to transfer all real estate to the Trust

- Fail to convey business interests to the Trust

- Create new accounts after the Trust is created, but open the accounts in an individual capacity instead of as Trustee

- Purchase new real estate after the Trust is created, but take title in an individual capacity instead of as Trustee

- Become entitled to funds that are payable individually, such as an inheritance or a tax refund, but not collect the funds or place them into a Trust account before death

The revocable Trust is often used to avoid probate. Probate is necessary whenever assets have not been placed into a Trust. Because of the likelihood that some assets may not be put into the Trust, a pour-over Will should be in place to put that property in the Trust.

A pour-over Will should generally:

- Nominate an Executor

- Name a Guardian, if you have minor children

- Identify the revocable Trust with specificity, referring to the title of the Trust, the date of its execution, the name of its creator, and the name of the initial Trustee

- Direct the entire estate to the Trustee of the revocable Trust

- Be entirely consistent with the revocable Trust agreement

Revocable Trusts are powerful planning tools, but they should only be utilized if you are specifically seeking the benefits they provide and are willing to commit the time and resources to establish, manage, and operate them properly.

Irrevocable Trusts

An irrevocable Trust, once established, cannot be easily changed or terminated. Assets, once placed in the Trust, don't typically come back out of it.

The decision to place assets in an irrevocable Trust is often driven by a desire to get assets out of your name on a formal basis, and protect them for the benefit of others. For example, I've had select clients who have set up an irrevocable Trust to benefit their children, knowing that they could then act freely with the assets retained in their name. This might be done by an aggressive investor who wants to set aside profits before continuing to seek further gain, almost like taking chips off a poker table.

If you get sued, assets placed in an irrevocable Trust are typically safe from creditors. If you try to qualify for government aid programs, assets placed in an irrevocable Trust aren't counted against you for purposes of qualification. You lose ownership and certain control of the assets, but gain protection against creditors.

A special type of irrevocable Trust can help a person avoid spending all of their money before entering a nursing home as required in the Medicaid nursing home spend-down provisions.

Assets in an irrevocable Trust are not subject to inheritance tax, but care must be taken in the case of life insurance to avoid includability.

The irrevocable Trust is a tax-efficient way to transfer accumulated wealth to beneficiaries. Like a revocable Trust, assets in an irrevocable Trust also avoid probate.

Appointing an independent Trustee is an important part of an irrevocable Trust. The law has strict regulations on Trustees that include having to account for benefits the Trustee may gain directly or indirectly from a Trust.

A Trustee is subject to many rules:

- A Trustee cannot use Trust property for private advantages. The Trustee will be held personally liable to account for profits made if this obligation is breached.

- A Trustee must use their power in the best interest of the beneficiaries of the Trust.

- A Trustee must manage a Trust with proper care. If the Trustee does not, they are held personally liable and will be required to compensate the beneficiaries.

It is important to know the differences between revocable and irrevocable Trusts to utilize them effectively for your estate planning, as every situation is different.

Another irrevocable Trust is one that's designated within your Will. Once you die, it springs into effect. These are known as *testamentary* Trusts and we'll cover various types of them in the upcoming pages.

WHEN

Trusts are frequently considered when you want to protect someone (beneficiaries or assets, like a minor child or someone with special needs) or something (substantial assets or wealth, since people without wealth rarely utilize a Trust).

Ideally, your attorney will help you set up the Trust document with language that does not need to be revisited frequently. However, certain life stages or milestones should prompt you to consider updating a Trust, such as:

1. Birth or death of a child, grandchild, or other beneficiary

2. Children or grandchildren reach age 18

3. Significant change in the asset value of the Trust

4. Divorce or marriage within the family

5. Retirement or other significant life event

Another consideration for when to revisit Trust allocations is in the event the value of the Trust's assets have changed. If property within the Trust has a fluid value, it will grow or shrink over time, and may affect your decisions to best support beneficiaries.

While a basic Trust document can be drawn up and executed in a single day, if you are hoping to use the Trust to shield assets from influencing Medicaid eligibility, there is a 5-year look-back window for that Federal program. Assets will need to have been held out of your name for 5 years – not part of your estate – for purposes of Medicaid analysis. If you're applying today for

Medicaid, but 4.5 years ago you gave away a piece of property valued at $200,000, then the government won't grant assistance until you spend or come up with that $200,000.

You will need to decide if the risk is worth the investment of setting up the Trust. Are you willing to pay an attorney to set up the Trust and a Trustee to keep assets safe and ensure you get the results you want?

"Give your children money so they feel they could do anything, but not so much that they could do nothing." —Warren Buffett

WHY

There are many options when it comes to the purpose and use of Trusts. For example, a charitable remainder Trust is where you set up the Trust but retain its benefits while you're alive. Then once you die, what's left goes to fund a charity of your choice. We will explore charitable giving in detail in Chapter Nine.

Here are some other options for Trust planning noted below.

TESTAMENTARY TRUSTS

A testamentary Trust is one that is created as part of the Will and only comes into effect upon your death. This option is good for those who do not want all assets to go outright to beneficiaries, but for whom the up-front costs of creating a separate Trust are prohibitive.

The provisions of testamentary Trusts can be changed while you are alive, and only become irrevocable upon your death. They are typically less complicated than setting up a free-standing Trust.

They are another way to provide greater post-death control of assets, such as in specific circumstances noted below.

For Minor Beneficiaries

A Will can create testamentary Trusts for any minor who otherwise would inherit property under the Will. A Trustee manages the investment and distribution of the inheritance for the minor's health, education, and maintenance over time. Once all money has been distributed, the Trust terminates.

As an example, if you die and leave your children $3M in the Will, the Guardian will hold the money until your kids reach age 18. The benefit of a Trust, with a designated Trustee, is that it can delay receipt of those funds even longer, releasing them at specific ages, or under specific conditions. I don't know about you, but if I would have received a substantial sum of money at age 18, I may not have made the best choices... *think Corvette.*

Typically, a Trust is set up to allow a portion of assets to be used for the benefit of the child on an ongoing basis, with the principal to be issued at certain designated times. One common manner is to issue one-third of the principal when the child reaches age 25, one-third at age 30, and the remainder at age 35.

When there is more than one child, you can opt for a pooled Trust for all children, or individual Trusts which may be customized for each child. These can provide distributions at varying times or ages, or at the discretion of the Trustee.

For families with multiple children, one of whom was gifted or loaned money while a parent was still alive, some choose to designate funds or an account to benefit the remaining children at equivalent dollar values.

Trusts in Action

Margaret is looking at options to designate funds to pass to her five children. Using a Will, she could stipulate that each child receive a certain percentage or fixed dollar amount. The money would pass to each child through probate as a one-time fixed sum. Using a Trust, however, it is possible to stipulate that each child receive a portion of their money at certain ages, or over the course of a number of years.

For example, each of the five children might be allotted $10k annually, which would draw down the Trust by $50,000, while the total value of the assets of the Trust can continue to accrue. Funds can be disbursed annually, bi-annually, or over any designated period of years.

If you've heard the term "trust fund baby," it typically refers to a beneficiary who receives annual installments from the Trust of someone who died.

A benefit of this method is that it shields the tax consequences of inheriting a large sum of money all at once. It also provides some protection in the case of failed marriages for a beneficiary. If one of Margaret's children is involved in a divorce, the remainder of the Trust assets are shielded from any settlement proceedings.

For Irresponsible Beneficiaries
Sometimes beneficiaries cannot responsibly handle their own financial affairs. In those situations, you can use a testamentary Trust to help protect the inheritance while still giving a Trustee the ability to make payments from the Trust assets for the person's support.

This can allow a Trustee discretion to delay any required distributions from the Trust for valid and significant reasons (such as for claims against the beneficiary, a dissolving marriage, or if the beneficiary is a defendant in litigation), or the Trust can be drafted so there are no required distributions at all.

For Retirement Accounts

Some retirement accounts with required minimum distributions, such as traditional IRAs, give an individual beneficiary the right to withdraw distributions over time, rather than taking one lump sum. Stretching out distributions can result in significant income tax savings to the beneficiary.

An account owner can use a testamentary Trust to take the lump-sum option away from the beneficiary, which is particularly useful if the beneficiary does not carefully manage finances. Stretching out the distributions over the beneficiary's lifetime is allowed if the Trust is drafted carefully and calls for the Trustee to pay out a required minimum distribution immediately to the beneficiary.

To Encourage Beneficiary Milestones

Testamentary Trusts can be used to control or incentivize behavior. For example, a Trust could pay educational and living expenses for a beneficiary while in school, with a lump sum distribution only upon graduation.

In these cases, you should name contingent beneficiaries in case the initial beneficiary does not satisfy the conditions to receive the lump sum distribution. If used, the Trust should set out clear standards to be met to receive the funds.

To Implement Estate Tax Planning

Testamentary Trusts can be set up to maximize estate tax savings or to avoid the estate tax altogether.

To Protect Beneficiaries in Non-Traditional Families

A testamentary Trust can be used to protect a significant other in a couple that chooses not to legally marry. A Trust can also be used for the benefit of a spouse or partner when you have children from other relationships, while still retaining the Trust remainder for your children.

To Preserve Property
You can create a Trust to keep specific property in the family. For example, a family cabin can be transferred to a Trust for the benefit of children and grandchildren, with the Trust terms dictating the manner in which the property should be maintained and how beneficiaries should share time at the location.

A Trust to Hold Property

One of my clients owns multiple farms in Southcentral Pennsylvania. He envisions the Trust will hold the property after he dies, and the money produced by all those farms can continue to benefit his beneficiaries. To ensure the success of those farms, however, a designation of the Trust should allow the Trustee(s) to invest money for the maintenance or repair of certain Trust assets, even extending to using Trust assets as collateral against a loan to cover costs.

For Out-of-State Real Property
My clients, Don and Linda, purchased a home on the shore of Deep Creek Lake, Maryland. This beautiful location offers activities on the lake in the summer and skiing at nearby resorts in the winter. When they purchased the property in their individual names, they realized it might be beneficial for them to put the property into a Trust.

They had two primary goals. First, they wanted the property to be owned by an entity that could be passed to one or more of their three sons, if any had an interest in owning and managing it. They knew a Trust could also allow ownership to be passed further to grandchildren someday. Second, they recognized that placement of the real estate in the Trust would avoid the need for an ancillary probate proceeding in Maryland, if and when they died as residents of the Commonwealth of

Pennsylvania. In this case, Don and Linda had a couple of objectives, and they used the Trust that accomplished them.

For Creditor Protection Benefits

A spendthrift Trust is designed to prevent a beneficiary's creditors from having any claim to Trust property until the property is actually distributed to the beneficiary. Spendthrift protection does have some limitations, including in the case of a beneficiary facing judgments for unpaid child support, spousal support, and government claims.

Supplemental or Special Needs Trusts

A supplemental or special needs Trust is designed for a beneficiary who is, or may later be, on a needs-based government entitlement program, such as Supplemental Security Insurance or Medicaid, because of disability. With properly drafted third-party special needs Trust provisions in the Will, assets passing into such a Trust do not disqualify the beneficiary from receiving public assistance.

Generation-Skipping Trust

This type of Trust allows you to leave property to grandchildren and other descendants while planning for the generation-skipping transfer tax and associated exemptions. This allows you to provide for multiple generations without incurring a transfer tax at each generational level.

Charitable Trust

With certain types of charitable Trusts, the estate can take a charitable deduction on the federal estate tax return. A charitable Trust can allow either:

- Non-charitable beneficiaries to receive a stream of income from the Trust for a period of time, with the Trust property ultimately going to a charity

- A charity to receive a stream of income for a period of time, with the Trust property ultimately going to non-charitable beneficiaries

Pet Trust

A Trust may also be set up to ensure care of a beloved pet. This Trust has a few functions. One is to designate a continued lifestyle to include veterinary care, food, and grooming. The other function is to provide funding to ensure this can be sustained.

Providing for a Pet

Casey has no living siblings, parents, or children, but owns a 10-year-old Akita dog who is well loved. Rather than being relegated to an animal shelter or euthanized upon Casey's death, she could set up a pet Trust that would allow the Akita to be more easily placed in a new home. The Trust could fund the animal's care and upkeep, including veterinary costs.

The SPCA has a program called Peace of Mind where, in the event of your death, they will complete medical checks for your pet and give your beloved animal concierge service and placement. All it requires is a one-time lump sum donation to the organization. In the event your pet dies before you, the service is transferable to another pet.

> ### Consider Percentages Rather than Fixed Amounts
>
> A client, Michael, had parents who were substantial investors. After their death, references to multiple dated Trusts were found, although only two could be located. The latest – from 20 years prior – allocated money to five siblings at different dollar amounts. Two were to receive $180,000 each, two would receive $140,000, and the final child would receive $100,000.
>
> Unfortunately the Trust was never updated when the assets' value increased. Because there was $2.5M in Trust assets at the time of the second parent's death, after giving the stipulated amounts to all the children, the way the Trust was worded, the favorite child got whatever was left. So essentially, one child received nearly $2M while the others benefitted far less.
>
> The pitfall here was stipulating strict dollar amounts. Those figures did not carry the right magnitude after the passage of time. In other cases, the value of assets may become reduced, and any designated dollar amount can cripple a fund as it must be paid first. For example, if you set up a Trust at age 65 when you're worth $5M, and you designate a charitable gift of $1M... but over time, expenses erode the fund – to where, at age 85, you have only $1M remaining – that $1M gift will be drawn out first from the Trust and there will be nothing left for other beneficiaries.

How

To draft a revocable Trust in Pennsylvania, you need to:

- Designate if it is a shared or individual Trust.

- Choose what property or assets to place in the Trust and designate parameters for how that property or assets should be treated. For example, how real estate should be used and maintained. Monetary assets might be placed in certain investment types.

- List Trust beneficiaries and how the Trust will be used for their benefit. Consider what time or life event distributions of Trust funds will take place.

- Name a Trustee who will follow your directives.

- Create the document with the assistance of an attorney.

- Sign the document in the presence of a Notary.

- Remember to sign the title of any Trust property with a title document that shows you own the property as Trustee of the Trust.

A Trust document doesn't need to be complicated, but it does need to be properly drafted. The Trust itself also needs to be maintained over time so that assets are titled to the Trust.

CAUTIONARY TALES

Don't forget to transfer assets into the name of the Trust. Even after all the setup costs and administrative effort to create the Trust, it is not uncommon to see people fail to properly title assets to that Trust before their death.

Christopher and Heidi had spent considerable time and money developing their Living Trust and related documentation, all of which exceeded 100 pages. However, there was one important, final step they had neglected to complete. Assets still needed to be conveyed into it.

Listing an asset in a Schedule attached to the Trust is not enough. For real property, you still must retitle the assets into the name of the Trust – preparing, signing and recording a new deed. For assets such as bank accounts or stocks, accounts must also be retitled in the name of the Trust at the financial institutions where they are held.

2 Do you actually need to set up a Trust while you are still alive, or can you use a testamentary Trust as part of your Will instead?

A Trust often costs $2,000 to $3,000 to set up, but can run as high as $10,000 depending on the complexity. If you invest $10,000, along with all the time and worry, and then eventually do not require Medicaid care, or certain tax benefits no longer apply, it's hard to justify having spent the money in the first place.

The bottom line? When approaching Trusts, consider what's most important to you. Do you want control? Do you want to avoid certain tax or healthcare liabilities? Can you trust that your beneficiaries will use your gifts in a manner in which you approve?

3 Individuals often spend time and effort to have a Trust created, but it is the wrong type of Trust to actually attain the desired goals.

Jacob and Mary had formed a Trust, hoping to shelter assets from the cost of long-term healthcare, like nursing home costs or fees associated with assisted living. Unfortunately, the individual with whom they met provided them with a Living Trust, which was revocable. This does not sufficiently distance assets from the owners in such a way that they would not count toward the cost of care.

Jacob and Mary had a *Living Trust*, when in fact they needed an *Irrevocable Trust*. It is very important to understand the goals being sought and confirm that the Trust, or other documents, are the right ones to achieve that goal. Be absolutely certain that you have the right estate planning documents for your situation, and ensure that they are set up properly to do what you need them to do. Don't find yourself in an estate planning horror story.

4 With the prevalence of second and third marriages these days, using specific Trust language and allocations, assets can be retained within family bloodlines. For example, the spouse who brings more money to the marriage may provide in his or her Will that money be put in a Trust upon death to benefit the surviving spouse. While the money in Trust can provide support to the surviving spouse, that person does not have control over the money. When the second spouse dies, the assets pass to the biological children of the spouse who died first. Trust funds can also be set up generationally, to children and grandchildren (though often not to wives or girlfriends).

Let's face it. People make bad decisions. Trusts and Trust language can be used to help avoid painful financial lessons for your beneficiaries.

OUT OF THE SPOTLIGHT

Some people use a Trust as a mechanism to maintain privacy. Because Wills become public record, if there is an asset or a magnitude of assets that you don't wish to become public knowledge, a Trust will shield that from being publicly noted during probate. One possible situation might be a person making allocations inside a Trust for the future care of an illegitimate child.

MAKE DOCUMENTS
ACCESSIBLE

SET GOALS

ABSOLVE FAMILY
OF BURDEN

S.M.A.R.T.

RELIEVE CHAOS
& CONFUSION

TAKE CARE OF

LOVED ONES

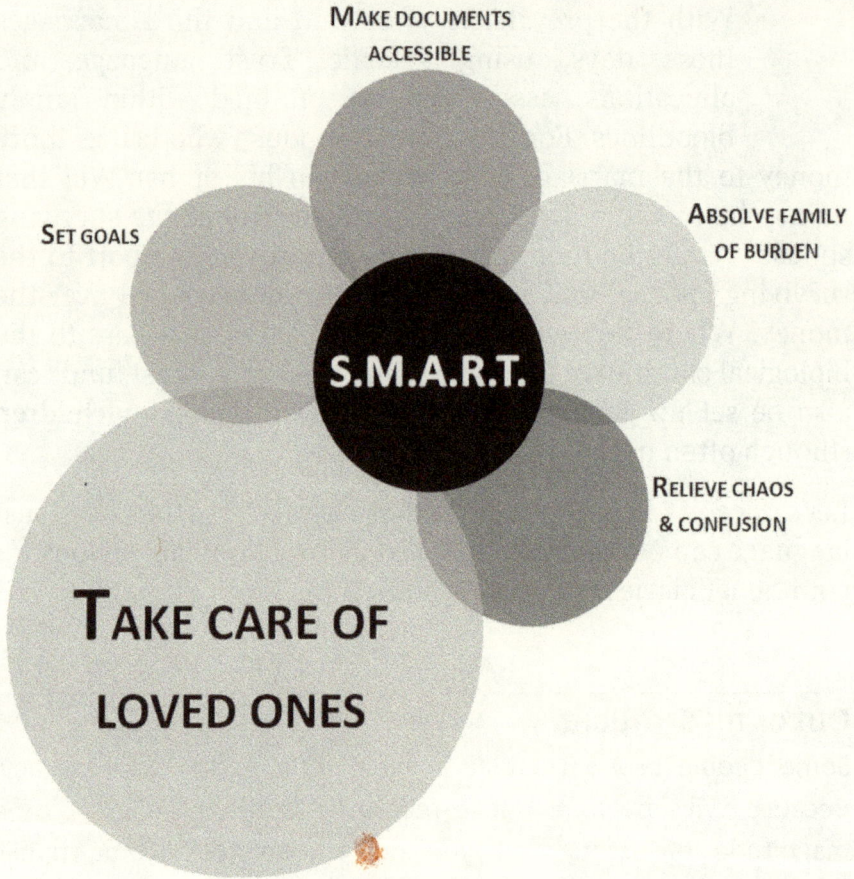

How can you **TAKE CARE OF LOVED ONES** even after you're gone?

☐ Consider who could benefit from having funds placed in a **Trust** rather than bequeathed outright in the Will.

☐ Consider who to name as **Trustee** for any funds placed in Trust to benefit your loved ones or charity.

☐ Make an appointment with trusted counsel to begin preparing the **Last Will & Testament**.

☐ Begin to shift assets into the name of the **Trust** to ensure your final wishes can be fulfilled.

7
FINAL INSTRUCTION LETTER

The process of making final arrangements can extend beyond the preparation of your Power of Attorney, Advance Healthcare Directive, Last Will and Testament, and setting up a Trust. It is often beneficial to prepare a letter for family or other loved ones that includes information about your funeral wishes, the location of important documents, and login credentials to necessary websites for accounts.

In recent months, I've attended three funerals and a wedding. While that may bring to mind the romantic comedy with Hugh Grant and Andie MacDowell, *Three Weddings and a Funeral,* these events served as reminders that not every eulogy speaker has the ability – especially while wracked with grief – to compile meaningful family stories or a list of the deceased loved one's life accomplishments, philosophies, and legacy. Nor do clergy have the benefit of a Hollywood screenwriter's help.

This same Final Instruction Letter can also contain personal stories or words of wisdom that will assist those who lead or participate in the funeral service. Clergy and funeral directors are well-versed at helping loved ones through this difficult time, but the addition of even just a few anecdotes or individual achievements will allow them to more easily paint a picture of all that shaped the deceased as a person.

FUNERAL ARRANGEMENTS

The best way to let your loved ones know about your funeral wishes is to write down a list of specific instructions in a document that is *separate* from your Will or Trust.

In many cases, funeral arrangements are made quickly, even before the Will has been located, since the probate process requires a death certificate to have been issued.

This instruction letter should detail what should (and should not) be done in regard to your funeral arrangements, so your family does not have to guess about your wishes.

The type of information to record in this document includes:

- Whether you want a funeral or a memorial service

- Where the service should be held

- Who should be specifically notified of your death

- Whether you want to be cremated or buried

- If cremated, where you would like your ashes stored, spread, or buried

- If money has been set aside to pay for funeral expenses – such as a life insurance policy for that purpose, or pre-paid arrangements – indicate where this information is located

In addition to a traditional written document, there are numerous online services for funeral pre-planning.

As with all estate planning, I recommend you have discussions with your loved ones about your final wishes. In this conversation, you may also let them know the location of your written documents. Often if something is only discussed verbally, it can be subject to misinterpretation or forgotten, so documentation is key to making your wishes known and easing the future burden for your loved ones.

Kim Butcher

Retired Funeral Director

"You don't have to wait until the last minute to arrange the funeral. Years ago, we didn't talk about death. Nobody wanted to sit around the kitchen table and say, 'You know, I'm gonna die someday and this is what I would like.' It was just taboo, but I recommend people take the opportunity to bring your family together. Let them know what your wishes and desires are. There's nothing worse than family making arrangements, looking at each other and saying, 'Well, I thought Dad told you what he wanted,' but nobody knows. Even if you don't want to have that serious talk, at least give your family the opportunity to have that information.

We don't want our families to have to suffer any undue burden. It's the ultimate gift that you can give them in realizing that they are upholding your final wishes in coordination with what they want.

No family has ever come to me and said, 'I wish Mom and Dad wouldn't have pre-planned their funeral.' You can do that even without pre-paying."

FOR THE OBITUARY

Your Final Instruction Letter can also include details about your life that would normally become part of the obituary notice.

This frequently entails your place and date of birth, your parents' names and locations (if still living), information about your education and certifications, any awards and significant accomplishments you received, hobbies and interests, organizational membership, church membership, and any military service. Many times the obituary will identify a charity that was significant to you in case others want to donate to it in your memory.

HELPFUL PROFESSIONALS

The next item to include is contact information for the helpful professionals whose services may come in handy to your loved ones in the months and years to come.

These include your attorney, accountant, financial planner, insurance agent, pension administrator, and any Trustee set up to manage assets placed in one or more Trusts.

LOCATION OF IMPORTANT PAPERS

At some point in the days and weeks following your death, loved ones will need access to many documents, insurance policies, and accounts.

In this section of the Final Instruction Letter, you can include the location of information like the following: Last Will and Testament, life insurance policies, health insurance policies, securities/investments, property deeds and/or mortgage statements, vehicle titles, retirement plan [401(k), pension, other], safe deposit box key, bank accounts, business agreements, and income tax returns.

Additionally, it can be useful to note the location of your birth certificate, marriage certificate, passport, firearm licenses, checkbook, and credit cards.

INTENTIONS FOR CHILDREN/GRANDCHILDREN

The next section of the document allows you to offer your intentions for children and grandchildren.

Do you envision they will attend college or a special training course? Have you set aside financial provisions for this foreseeable future?

This is also a place where you can share any specific intentions you have for their wedding(s). Is there a family heirloom that has been designated to pass on the occasion of a wedding, or other arrangements your loved ones should know about?

LIST OF MAJOR ASSETS

In the next section of this document, list any major assets your loved ones should be aware of. Include things like stocks and bonds, real estate, insurance policies, retirement accounts, bank accounts (including money market accounts and CDs), and major personal effects (such as jewelry, art, antiques). A benefit of this section is to identify assets that loved ones might not know about. For example, if you own property in a different state or country, or a financial asset like an interest in a partnership, this could be noted in the Final Instruction Letter.

FINAL DETAILS

In the final section, include the bank location and pertinent information for any safe deposit box, details about any liabilities (more than $2,000), and the location of a list of login credentials and passwords for online accounts.

Your loved ones may express concern about not knowing how to pay all the bills in the days immediately following your death. Most companies have lenient policies related to debt collection when someone has died. In many cases, a copy of the death certificate will be required to enact a name change on the account, so let your family know it is generally okay to sit on any bills until the estate opens.

SHARING THIS DOCUMENT

A common question once people complete this and other essential documents is:

"Do I give these to my kids?"

My advice typically is... if they're helping you now, then give the documents to them. If they're not doing something for you (for example, paying bills, or balancing accounts), then just place the document somewhere safe and let them know where it is.

CAUTIONARY TALES

1 As soon as the obituary hits the news, there is a potential for scammers to reach out to loved ones, pretending to be creditors. The Final Instruction Letter can help your family members avoid being duped by people with fraudulent intent, as your loved ones can have a better understanding of all your legitimate accounts and activity.

2 Don't put off creating your file of important documents. You don't have to have everything perfectly organized to start, but both you and your loved ones will benefit from making those items more easily accessible.

3 Don't forget about your digital pictures! With the rise in usage of cell phone cameras, many of us no longer have printed photographs stored in physical albums. Since one spouse or family member might have a bunch of family pictures that others do not have, it is important to let someone know how to access those images.

MAKE DOCUMENTS
ACCESSIBLE

SET GOALS

ABSOLVE FAMILY
OF BURDEN

S.M.A.R.T.

RELIEVE CHAOS
& CONFUSION

TAKE CARE OF

LOVED ONES

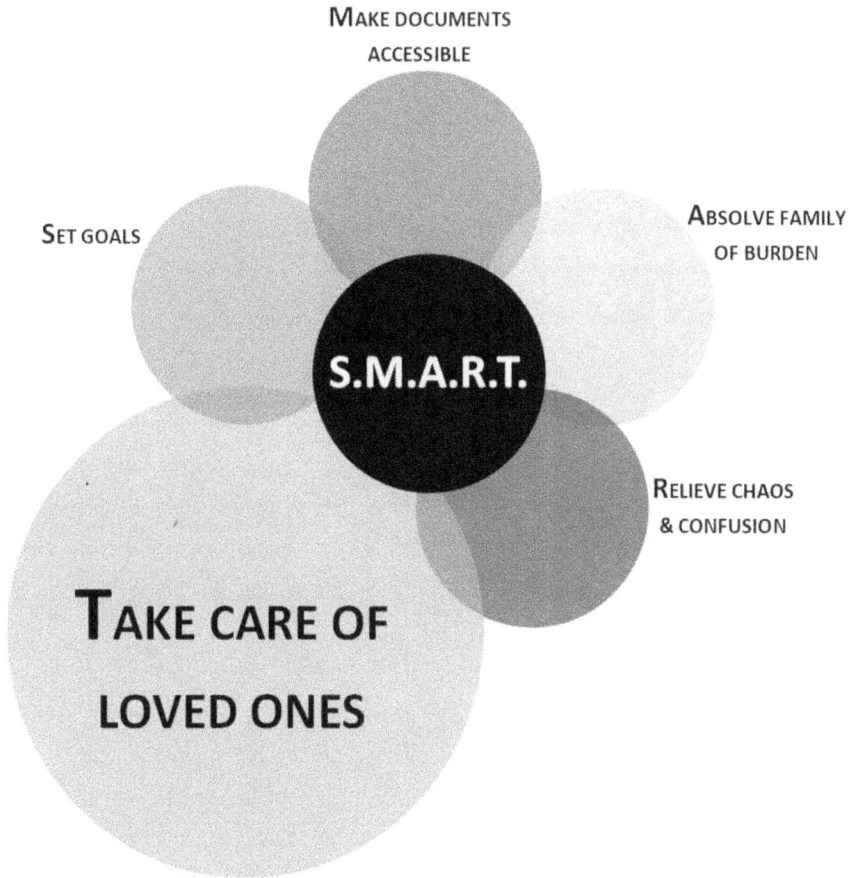

Yet another way you can **TAKE CARE OF LOVED ONES** even after you're gone:

☐ Prepare a **Final Instruction Letter** that includes a list of contacts and information that will be needed in the hours and days immediately following death.

In Appendix C, I have provided a sample Final Instruction Letter (see page 221), along with advice on which documents you should keep in the vicinity of this letter.

8 DEATH AND PROBATE

Following the death of a loved one, there are many steps which must be taken, not the least of which is grieving your loss. If you do not have family and friends who can offer emotional support, consider contacting a bereavement group so you do not have to feel so alone.

Among the first items you will face is notifying family, friends, and employers, as well as any clergy. A section of the Final Instruction Letter from the previous chapter will simplify this task if contact information is already gathered and consolidated into one place.

Arrangements will need to be made with a funeral home, which typically include an obituary listing, the preparation of your loved one's body, a visitation, a memorial service, and burial or cremation.

In addition to information for the obituary, you should also gather financial information, such as life insurance or burial policies, as well as written wishes for how any memorial service should be conducted. If your loved one served in the military, remember to bring the honorable discharge papers.

Consider contacting a bereavement group so you do not have to feel so alone.

When you reach out to make an appointment to visit the funeral home, they will inform you of a list of items to bring, including photographs, a list of special songs or hymns, and clothing for the deceased. Typically the funeral home will also assist you in filing for copies of the death certificate, and reporting the death to Social Security.

"HOW CAN I HELP?"

During your time of loss, it is normal for others to want to support you, but it can be difficult for them to know specific items or tasks that might be helpful.

While there are many items you will want to handle yourself, some ideas for things that could be delegated include:

- Preparing food

- Creating a photo collage for the memorial service

- Caring for pets or plants

- Mowing the lawn and other routine household chores

- Making phone calls

- Helping with arrangements for out-of-town guests

- Reminding you to drink water and take any necessary medications

- Watching over young children during funeral planning or at the service

- Keeping an eye on the home when unoccupied, to prevent theft

- Addressing thank you cards

Delegating certain tasks to others not only lightens your load, but it also allows them to feel like they are helping you in some way. This can be a comfort to you both during such a stressful time.

Jack Sommer
Former CEO, Prospect Hill / Greenmount Cemeteries & Cremation Gardens

"Cemeteries really are for the living. The human need is to be remembered and to remember.

Decisions run the full spectrum of traditional ground burial to cremation and dealing with the cremated remains. There are so many choices. You can have your remains spun into glass and made into beautiful objects for your family.

We are the only cemetery in York County with an ossuary. Scattering cremated remains is not typically permitted, but an ossuary provides a place of permanence where the cremated remains of family can be kept.

In the absence of decisions, people just kind of freeze. The real value of a cemetery is to guide families through the decision matrix and give the information they need to make an informed decision, one that they're comfortable with.

Though talking with professionals and then making some decisions will require you to address or acknowledge your own mortality, once your decisions are properly recorded, you can put these thoughts aside and know that someone else can carry forward these instructions. You will have provided a roadmap. All someone else has to do is follow the roadmap."

AFTER THE FUNERAL

The days immediately following the death of a loved one can feel like a whirlwind of activity. You may find yourself at times surrounded by people and longing for a moment of solitude. However, after a week of pressing demands and public gatherings, there usually follows a period of time that can be equally challenging, as you face the task of collecting legal documents and preparing for probate.

You will also want to review any outstanding bills and, if possible, keep them current. If you are unable to make timely payments, reach out to any creditors and explain the situation. Most are happy to offer a grace period.

If you haven't already, during this time you can reach out to your loved one's employer to inquire about any wage and death benefits, like unused sick or vacation pay, unpaid commissions, credit union balances, pension funds, and group life insurance.

> Leonard worked for Northrup Grumman. His wife had to open an estate because he had accrued so much paid time off that it couldn't be passed directly to her but had to go to his estate. The lesson is to be mindful of unique assets and try to plan around them. When the amount of accrued time became noticeably large, perhaps he could have taken a payout to reduce its value, which would have avoided the need for an estate.

Legal documents you will want to compile include:

- Last Will and Testament
- Insurance policies
- Property and vehicle titles
- Bank and credit card account information, including loans and mortgages
- Investment account information
- Death certificate

At this time, you may choose to reach out to an attorney for assistance. Unless it's the simplest of estates, an attorney can likely provide assistance and value in addressing matters, taking the burden of legal paperwork and notices off of your shoulders.

If the estate is particularly complex or you foresee challenges or struggles among beneficiaries, it can be a comfort to have the help of objective counsel as a third-party, capable of mediating any issues. It can also be helpful to engage an attorney if your loved one held property in multiple states or countries, or if there are extenuating circumstances like a lost or destroyed Will.

PROBATE

WHO

The **Decedent** is the person who died.

A **Personal Representative** (**Executor/Executrix** if identified in a Will) is the individual authorized to administer the estate.

More than one person can be designated **Executor** either acting together (both signatures required), or separately (only one or the other signature required).

An **Administrator** is the **Personal Representative** appointed by the court when someone dies without a Will.

A **Guardian** is a person designated to provide physical care for children and/or pets.

A **Trustee** is a person designated to administer the wishes of the deceased as expressed through a Trust document.

OPENING THE ESTATE

In Pennsylvania, the filing is made with the Register of Wills in the County where the deceased resided. Typically you contact the Register's office and provide documentation, then schedule an appointment.

The Personal Representative is the one who must appear. If the Decedent died with a Will, an original of the document must be filed with the Register. If there is no Will, then there will be other documentation to prepare.

For estates with a total value less than $50,000, you may be eligible to use an abbreviated proceeding known as Settlement of Small Estate on Petition. This can be used whether or not your loved one had a Will.[7]

In instances where the designated Personal Representative is in military service, has a conflict of interest, or in any other situation is not available to serve, someone can be appointed temporary Personal Representative, again, whether or not the person died with a Will in place.

The initial filing will likely include:

- Original Will and any Codicils

- Death certificate

- Petition for grant of letters

- Estate information sheet (a few Pennsylvania counties do not require this)

---

[7] If a Pennsylvania resident dies with property not exceeding $50,000, exclusive of real property and certain property payable to family and funeral directors, any interested party may petition the Orphans' Court to direct distribution of the estate without a full estate administration proceeding. Local practice varies, so consult the Register's office for further information.

- Filing fees (vary by county, as does the time in which each fee is charged)

- Bond, if required

- Any renunciations with witnesses to those (for example, if multiple children were named Executor, but some live far away or feel unable to serve for some other reason)

- Other documents may be necessary, especially if there was no Will

If the Decedent died with a Will but the original is unavailable, a photocopy may be probated by filing a petition. This will however require proof of two witnesses to attest to the proper execution of the Will, and clear and convincing evidence that the content of the unavailable original Will is substantially the same as set out in the copy being probated.

If the Decedent died without a Will, letters of administration may be granted in the following order of priority:

- Surviving spouse

- Those entitled under intestate law to receive the estate assets

- The Decedent's principal creditors

- Other fit persons, as determined by the court

- The guardianship support agency serving as Guardian of an incapacitated individual who dies during the guardianship

WHO IS ENTITLED TO RECEIVE NOTICE?
Unlike a scene from an Agatha Christie tale or the recent movie *Knives Out,* there is rarely a "reading of the Will" in which family members and other interested parties are all present. Typically, written notification is provided instead.

Within three months of appointment, the Personal Representative must give notice to each person who is entitled to inherit.
This includes all named beneficiaries, as well as the Decedent's
spouse and children – regardless of whether they are named in
the Will.

Notice must also be given to the Trustee of any Trusts, any
charitable beneficiary whose interest exceeds $25,000, as well
as the office of the Attorney General. For any minor beneficiary
or incapacitated beneficiary, the appointed Guardian must be
notified.

In addition to notifying the specific people named above, the
grant of letters must be advertised in one newspaper with
general circulation in the area where the Decedent resided, as
well as the legal newspaper designated by local rule. This notice
must be published once a week for a period of three consecutive
weeks. Creditors will have a period of one year from the first
complete advertisement of the grant of letters to recover claims.
After that one-year period, a creditor can only recover if the
Personal Representative receives the claim before distribution
of assets is made.

ADMINISTERING THE ESTATE

Your main duties as Personal Representative are to first gather
and secure the estate assets, then administer and distribute
them. One of the first steps to administering the estate is to
obtain an Employer Identification Number (EIN) – think of it
like a Social Security Number for the estate.

In almost every case, a checking account is opened in the name
of the estate, using its EIN. That account can be opened at the
same bank used by your deceased loved one, or at a bank more
convenient to you. This account is where funds should be
gathered to pay debtors, and eventually, distribute assets to
beneficiaries.

If there is a home that is now unoccupied, make sure the house and any valuables are secure. If the property needs to be sold, consider what needs to be done to sell at a favorable price. For example, think about what personal property needs to be given to beneficiaries, sold to a third party, or simply discarded. Many times, someone in the family will want to buy the property, either as part of their gift as beneficiary or to purchase outright. If the property needs to be sold beyond the family, you can decide whether it makes sense to engage a realtor.

For items that must be valued or appraised, rather than liquidated, keep a file listing the amounts. In most cases creditors will not request to see actual appraisals, so it is often sufficient to make rough estimates. For vehicles, the *Kelley Blue Book* value may be used, based on the car's current condition.

Estate assets might also include items that are difficult to identify or locate such as unclaimed property, savings bonds, or book entry stock. The Pennsylvania Treasurer maintains a website list of unclaimed property. A review of the most recent income tax return and property tax receipt can help identify assets.

Examples of assets to list on the inventory include:

- Real estate
- Bank accounts
- Vehicles, boats, and motor homes
- Jewelry, art, antiques, and home furnishings
- Stock and bonds
- Pension funds
- Unpaid holiday and sick leave

- Debts owed to the Decedent

- Interests in a partnership, sole proprietorship, limited liability company, or closely held corporation

- Oil, gas, or mineral rights

Decedents can have some assets that are not subject to probate, like a family home owned jointly with a right of survivorship. Only probate property is subject to the estate administration process, though non-probate property may be included as part of the estate for income tax, state inheritance tax, or federal estate tax purposes.

After collecting and securing a catalog of assets (the estate inventory), you should file:

- Decedent's final income tax return(s)

- Pennsylvania Inheritance Tax Return (Form REV-1500)

- U.S. Estate Tax Return (Form 706), if necessary

Within three months of the Decedent's death, Pennsylvania inheritance tax may be prepaid to receive a 5 percent discount on the tax amount. For example, if the inheritance tax is $10,000, you could prepay and save $500. The tax return and inventory *must* be filed with the Register of Wills within nine months of the death.

You, as Personal Representative, should also use diligent efforts to identify and settle the Decedent's debts before distributing estate assets to the beneficiaries.

Before the final settlement of the estate and distribution of assets, you may make a partial distribution to one or more beneficiaries. For example, a beneficiary might ask you for an early portion of their inheritance to assist them with some personal goal like buying a car, paying off student debt, or purchasing a new home. Exercise caution in making such interim distributions. You need to ensure there are sufficient assets left to cover all the taxes, creditors, and expenses of administration. In the event you, as the Personal Representative, choose to make such early distributions, you will be liable to creditors for any claims against the estate.

CLOSING THE ESTATE

After the Inheritance Tax Return is filed, the Department of Revenue reviews it and issues a notice setting forth its determinations regarding the value of the estate assets, allowable deductions, and tax due. Depending upon the complexity of the Return, it can take about six months from the date the return is filed with the Register of Wills for processing to be completed. Ideally, the Inheritance Tax Return is accepted as filed, and all deductions are allowed. If the Return is not accepted as filed, then the Department of Revenue will issue a notice of determination that changes the amount of inheritance tax that must be paid (for example, by disallowing a deduction that was claimed, which would increase the tax amount). You may accept such a determination or appeal it within 60 days of receiving the notice.

Following the approval of the inventory, appraisement of the inheritance tax return, and satisfaction or resolution of any outstanding claims and liabilities, the estate should be closed.

This can be done informally, by release agreement (often called a family settlement agreement) which is signed by any and all beneficiaries of the estate as well as the Personal Representative. Sometimes a formal filing of an account is necessary for the account to be approved by the court. Most estates are closed by release agreement, which does not require a court appearance. The release agreement allows the beneficiaries to approve the administration of the estate and consent to the distribution of assets. It also provides a release of the Personal Representative, which in essence protects this person from future liability.

A release agreement may not be an option – or may not be the best option to protect the Personal Representative – if the estate is insolvent, there are unsatisfied claims, or if beneficiaries or future beneficiaries of Trusts are unwilling to sign or cannot be adequately represented in the release agreement.

Regardless, once the administration of the estate is complete, the Personal Representative must file a final status report with the Register of Wills, informing that the administration is now complete and whether an account was filed with the court.

When tackling the final distribution of assets, it is in your best interest as Personal Representative to keep a detailed report of payments made and dates distributed, in addition to a record of accounts and bills, such as utilities, that may need to be updated to a different name going forward. The failure to update names on utilities could cause problems.

How Much

The primary costs of an estate proceeding in Pennsylvania include:

- Filing fees, including those for petition of grant of letters and inventory
- Legal notice or advertisement fees
- Taxes, including federal estate and generation-skipping transfer tax, income tax, and state inheritance tax (up to 15 percent of the taxable estate)
- Personal Representative compensation
- Accounting fees
- Attorney fees
- Bond fees

- Appraisal and valuation fees

- Real estate agent commissions, if selling real estate

- Auction fees, if selling personal property

The total expected costs will vary depending on the size and complexity of the estate, whether a bond is required, whether there are any challenges to the estate, and how involved a lawyer must be in matters of the estate.

WHEN

The typical length of time for opening and closing an estate varies with the nature and complexity of the estate. Other factors include the ease of locating beneficiaries, whether there are any challenges to the estate, and the volume of work the court has when the Will is offered for Probate.

The bulk of estate administration is usually completed in 5 to 9 months before the tax return is filed with the state. It is often 6 months before the state renders a decision on the tax return. In total, it may take one to two years to complete everything because of tax filing due dates. For example, if the Decedent died early in the year, the final income tax return may not be able to be filed until late the following year.

In regard to when to expect to handle certain steps, the following timeline offers a summary.

WITHIN 3 MONTHS OF DEATH

- Notify banks, employers, insurance companies, stock brokers, and begin identifying assets and liabilities.

- Arrange for your deceased loved one's mail to be forwarded.

- Advertise the grant of letters from the Register of Wills.

- Send required written notices to all beneficiaries under the Will and to heirs at law, with certification to the Register of Wills.

- Make advance payment of state inheritance tax, to qualify for a 5 percent discount.

WITHIN 6 MONTHS OF DEATH

- Estimate cash needed to pay all debts and taxes.

- Plan for the sale of any assets, like real estate or vehicles.

- Prepare and file inventory of the estate with the Register of Wills.

WITHIN 9 MONTHS OF DEATH

- Prepare and file state inheritance tax return.

- Prepare and file federal estate tax return, if needed.

- Prepare and file any other death tax returns for property located in other states or countries.

ADDITIONAL TASKS

Prepare and file your deceased loved one's final lifetime income tax returns for federal and state. These are due April 15 of the year following death.

Distribute assets from the estate. This can begin any time, but is usually concluded after death taxes have been settled.

Once the administration of the estate is complete and assets have been distributed, notice should be given to the Register of Wills through a status report.

CAUTIONARY TALE
A friend's father recently died. In his Will, the father named his attorney as Executor of the estate. The daughters performed all

the cleaning and preparation of the family home to list it for sale. Unfortunately, the attorney, who is now 85 years old, wants to charge a 7 percent fee on the sale of the home, and is also slow to process matters of the estate.

When considering someone for the position of Executor, make sure this person is not only well-qualified, but will also retain that capacity when called to serve. Be sure to establish or understand any fee structure that may be required.

WHEN IN DOUBT

Handling the legal paperwork and distribution of assets for your loved one can feel daunting. Even if the process is relatively straightforward based on the size of the estate, there are many steps that need to be taken care of in a timely manner.

While cleaning out the family home is a sizeable and very personal undertaking, delegating the legal paperwork of probate is one way to remove emotional and mental burden during what can be a stressful time.

Most of my clients rely on me to handle the documentation and legal matters, including notices, the inheritance tax return, and court filings. Unless you're absolutely confident in your ability to navigate these tasks, you may want to reach out to a trusted attorney for help when you need it.

9
CHARITABLE GIFTS

If a cause matters to you, how do you begin your search for how to give charitably? And to whom?

When it comes to charitable giving, I have found that some people prefer to do so through a mechanism like estate planning – so they are no longer concerned about how much money they will need for their own wellbeing – while others choose to make gifts during their lifetime.

A secondary concern is trying to determine how much money will be necessary for your children. Parents who feel like their kids need all their assets are less likely to make a charitable gift. Others are more comfortable with charitable gifts once they believe they have ample assets or feel their adult children will not need the money. I have had many clients say, "My son won't need the gift because he has a great job and has been very successful."

Unfortunately, too often, charitable giving falls by the wayside. People forget to include it when estate planning, or are too confused about the best way to get started.

However, you may be someone who already makes significant charitable contributions of money or time. In that case, your decision about which charitable organizations could benefit from gifts after your death may be more obvious. For example, if you routinely serve food at the pantry or your church, these agencies could also benefit from your financial philanthropy after death.

If you're not sure what you want to do with the money you've saved up, think about the legacy you want to leave. Ask yourself, "How do I want to be remembered?"

There are several avenues you can choose to help others through charitable giving as part of your estate plan.

NAME A CHARITY IN YOUR WILL

In addition to naming loved ones in your Will, like a spouse and children, you can name a charity as a beneficiary. As a side benefit, this kind of giving lowers the amount of your taxable estate.

Additionally, if something happens to you and your spouse and kids and grandkids – basically wiping out your core family – a *charitable gift-over* option in your Will would allow one or more charities to receive funds from your estate rather than those same assets following intestacy laws for distribution. Intestacy laws could result in distant relatives, with whom you have no real relationship, or even the state itself receiving assets.

> *Ask yourself, "How do I want to be remembered?"*

When naming charities in your Will, take the time to contact each charity or look at its website to make sure you identify it in a way that does not create confusion between two or more similarly named organizations. Also remember that many nonprofits have both national agencies as well as the local chapter or branch. If you want only your local office to receive your contribution, be sure to make specific note of that within your Will.

Often people will name a charity in the Will for which they have participated or donated during their lifetime. For example, one of our CGA Law staff members, Chris, routinely donates blood. To continue that legacy of giving, she could designate the American Red Cross as a beneficiary in her Will.

As you begin to think about causes that matter to you, consider schools you have attended. Many school districts, colleges, and universities have programs set up for charitable giving, including the ability to have your funds directed to certain areas like sports, music, theater, science, or even field trips. It is also possible to designate funds toward specific uses – like new marching band uniforms, or biology lab equipment – though this may limit the usefulness of the gift depending on current organizational needs.

Many of my clients identify gifts to schools. It might be your high school or college, or the school of one or more of your children. These gifts are often designated for scholarships. Dollars for Scholars® is frequently a recipient of such gifts. Other times, gifts are used to support athletics, activities, or educational programs.

In addition to your alma mater, consider organizations you have participated with in the past, perhaps serving on a board, fundraising, or volunteering. Also think about nonprofits that serve segments of the population you want to support. Common ones are the American Cancer Society, American Heart Association, the United Way, the Salvation Army, and the SPCA (both national and local).

 A former client, Jean, named multiple charities in her Will to receive $5,000 to $20,000 apiece—various camping ministries within her United Methodist church, her local Make-a-Wish Foundation, a Cancer Patient Help Fund of her local hospital, Doctors Without Borders, a sorority at her alma mater to assist with new furniture purchases, two hospice centers, and her local Appalachian Trail conference.

SET UP A CHARITABLE ROLLOVER FROM AN IRA

You can name a charity as an IRA beneficiary. It is also possible to make use of a charitable tax break while you are still alive.

You can donate up to $100,000 per year straight from an IRA, and that amount can even count toward any required minimum distributions. This allows you to exclude the charitable donation from your income so you don't pay taxes on it.

When gifting a charity as beneficiary of your IRA or other retirement accounts upon your death, rather than donating retirement assets during your lifetime, there are multiple benefits.

Estate planners often talk about "competing tax considerations." Should you give your house to a child before you die, or should they inherit it afterward? Many times you must choose between the lesser of two evils. In the case of charitable gifting of an IRA rollover, however, you actually can get multiple benefits. Upon your death the charity receives the assets and your beneficiaries will not have to pay the income taxes on that money. The gift itself essentially becomes a tax deduction for the estate, avoiding income tax and inheritance tax, and maximizing your gift to the charity.

SET UP A FOUNDATION, OR GIFT AN EXISTING FOUNDATION

A few of my past clients have set up their own foundations, but bear in mind that this is like setting up a business enterprise. You really need to be dedicated to the giving, and you will need to maintain this foundation both during and after your lifetime for it to remain viable and successful.

A far more straightforward option is working with a community foundation. You can set up your own named fund to create your charitable legacy. In the case of York County Community Foundation, YCCF handles all the paperwork. They do take a fee to cover that, but after this expense, you can decide how the monies should be used.

Typically you can gift any amount you like, to almost anyone you want, for however long you want. Community foundations are an option for both big and small donors to help structure your gifts for maximum impact and tax benefits.

Mary Kay Bernosky, Esq.
Vice President Development
York County Community Foundation

"We have various types of funds. Some are donor-advised, where the donor makes recommendations about where the funding goes annually. We have designated funds, where a donor stipulates tax-exempt entities, whether they be in York or anywhere else in the country that they want to support. Then we have our more unrestricted funds, which support needs within the community. We also work with the Dollars for Scholars organizations.

One of our donor families, the Andersons, created funds to support agriculture in the community, and they give out grants that are determined by a committee that looks at what the issues are and what applications are available.

We are one of the largest community foundations in Pennsylvania, just behind Philadelphia, Pittsburgh, and Erie. That says a lot about the generosity of the York community."

The goal of many community foundations is to build funds that will last in perpetuity. When you make a donation, the foundation commits to pay a certain percentage of that fund forever. For example, a $100,000 contribution can be held in reserve, paying out 5 percent each year... or $5,000 each and every year... without end.

Establishing a gift through a community foundation is a nice way to enjoy the benefits of having your legacy giving recognized during your lifetime, yet continue beyond your death.

Members of my firm, CGA Law, chose to create a named charitable fund within the York County Bar Foundation. Assets may be used to support activities of the Foundation such as legal aid, youth initiatives, advocacy, ethics and professionalism, and scholarships.

GIFT REAL ESTATE

Not all charitable giving has to be cash. Gifts of real estate – like a condo, vacation home, farm, or undeveloped land – can be utilized for the benefit of a charity. For example, a local nonprofit might raffle off entries to win a vacation week at a beachfront property throughout the year, with proceeds used to further the nonprofit's mission. Or a nonprofit that provides equestrian therapy for special needs children might open a satellite branch on a farm or ranch that comes through a donation.

A gift of real estate allows various ownership aspects. You can gift it outright, or reserve lifetime ownership for you and your spouse. It is also possible to achieve certain tax benefits from your donation.

Paul Smith, a Southern York County builder, donated several tracts of land to the Southern York County Library. Upon the sale of that land several years later, the dollar equivalent of his gift was enough to qualify for naming rights of the building, which is now known as Paul Smith Library of Southern York County.

GIFT APPRECIATED STOCK

Another popular gift is stock or other investments. If you've held them for a while, they typically have acquired substantial value. To sell them on your own and convert to cash, you will likely have tax implications. However, when you donate stock that's been held for more than one year, you not only make a difference charitably, but you can also avoid paying capital gains tax on the holdings, as it qualifies for long-term capital gains treatment.

George worked for a utility company for 30 years. He received stock as part of his compensation. When he retired, the stock generated income for him, via dividends. Upon his death, he gifted the stock to a community foundation for use with youth initiatives.

CREATE A CHARITABLE GIFT ANNUITY

A charitable gift annuity is a contract made with a charity. You gift a sizable portion of cash or other asset in exchange for a partial tax deduction for your donation, plus a fixed stream of income from the charity for the rest of your life.

Your gift is set aside in a reserve account and invested by the charity. Based on your age at the time of the gift (or the ages of you and your spouse if gifting jointly), a fixed monthly or quarterly amount that is supported by the investment account will be made to you.

At the end of your life (as well as your spouse's if making a joint gift), the charity will receive the remainder of the annuity.

Annie was a pharmacist who set aside $100,000 to fund an annuity for her local school district. While she was alive, it paid her $12,000 a year. Upon her death, the funds remaining in the annuity were donated to her alma mater and utilized to purchase equipment for the science department.

CREATE A CHARITABLE REMAINDER TRUST

A charitable remainder Trust allows you to retain access and benefits of Trust assets while you're alive. Once you die, what's left goes to fund a charity of your choice. As an incentive, most larger charitable organizations have a department or person who can help set this up for you. Using a charitable remainder Trust is a great way to make sure you're never short on money during your lifetime, while allowing the charitable organization to be aware of, and be ready to utilize, the gift effectively when the time is right.

Charitable remainder Trusts are more flexible and give you more asset control than charitable gift annuities, because you can name or be the Trustee, and change the charitable beneficiary over time. The downside is that a charitable remainder Trust is more complex to create and administer than a charitable gift annuity.

USE LIFE INSURANCE OR A CHARITABLE GIFT RIDER

Your loved ones can use proceeds from a life insurance policy to cover funeral and other expenses, however you can also name one or more charities as a beneficiary on your policy. Another option is a charitable giving rider, which pays a percentage of the policy's face value to a qualified charity, without reducing the cash value or death benefits of your policy, but they can limit how much you can gift this way.

All of these options allow you to help others through charitable giving as part of your estate plan. Some offer tax benefits during your lifetime, and some create tax benefits for your beneficiaries. Your choice is ultimately personal, and comes down to what assets and how much you would like to funnel to charity to benefit others.

The act of charitable giving is a wonderful extension of support for organizations you already value, or for causes you want to further.

As an added benefit, charitable giving elevates your own gratitude, which enhances your health, happiness, and optimism. It is also a way to help people in need, benefit your community, and strengthen new or existing friendships.

CAUTIONARY TALES

1 Remember to update your document when you are no longer involved with a charitable organization named in your Will. For example, if you named your hometown church as a beneficiary, but later moved away and now feel connected to a different congregation, consider whether you would like to shift your charitable giving, or even include both organizations instead.

2 Be mindful of how you identify gift amounts. Some people name fixed dollar amounts, while others designate percentages. If you identify fixed dollar amounts, you need to be mindful that your estate maintains enough money to pay out all your intended beneficiaries.

For example, if you gift $200,000 to charity with the assumption that your estate contains $1M, there will be $800,000 to go to beneficiaries that are not charitable, such as your loved ones. But if your estate later shrinks to $400,000, then a $200,000 gift to charity would represent half of your estate... leaving your other beneficiaries with only $200,000 to share.

A safer option would be to designate a percentage of your estate to be devoted to charitable gifts, rather than specific dollar amounts.

If you do utilize percentages, you still need to be mindful about the totality of your estate, as the actual amount of the gift will vary based on your estate size.

For example if your estate is $500,000 and you decide to gift 10 percent to charity, that's a $50,000 gift. However, if your estate increases to $2M then that same 10 percent gift grows to $200,000. You may or may not intend to make a gift of that size.

Savvy Tip: When choosing between fixed dollar amounts and percentages in the language of your bequest, you still need to understand what that will yield in real dollars. Another option is to designate "the lesser of" a specific dollar amount or percent of the estate. For example, "limit this bequest to the lesser of $25,000 or 10 percent of my estate."

3 Remember that estate planning doesn't need to occur all the time, but you do need to remain aware of your estate and circumstances to ensure your planning goals are met at any time and that there is not a disconnect between what your documents dictate and what you would actually prefer to give.

Super Savvy Tip: If you have concerns about how and when your charitable gift will be used by an organization, consider including language in your Will to guide their decision-making.

EX: "I bequeath ___ (amount) to ___ (organization), ___ (address), to be utilized as they deem appropriate; however, no more than Fifty (50) percent may be utilized for scholarships. The non-scholarship funds must be utilized within three (3) years of the date of my death or the bequest shall revert to my Estate and shall be distributed in accordance with Item (#) below. The Trustee established by this Will shall monitor the utilization of this gift during the three (3) year period, to confirm that it is utilized as I direct or to ensure that it is returned to my Estate."

10
WHEN YOUR CHILD TURNS 18

It is a very exciting time when your child graduates from high school and is ready to embark on the next stage of life. Who would believe that the person who possibly still relies on you for money and food and lodging would actually be an adult now with legal rights of their own?

Turning 18 is a critical milestone in estate planning, whether your child intends to work part-time or full-time, attend college, or even take a gap year to travel.

When your child becomes a legal adult, this carries a host of rights and responsibilities for them, and also limits your legal access to such things as their medical and financial records. Such legal protections and restrictions sometimes result in unintended consequences.

To help your adult child during the often tumultuous years ahead, you will need information. Unfortunately, the very laws that once protected your child's personal information from outsiders now block you from accessing it. Just imagine... one day you know everything and can make decisions in the best interests of your child, and the next day, your child has to sign paperwork to give *you* permission to help.

For example, once your child is a legal adult, in the event of a medical crisis, Health Insurance Portability and Accountability Act (HIPAA) rules prevent doctors and other care providers from speaking with you about the details of your child's condition, and banks and credit card companies will no longer share information about the state of accounts held solely in your child's name. You also may not be granted access to your child's college grades – even if you are the one paying tuition. Imagine you are paying all that money, but you don't even get a report card.

To ensure your continued ability to help your child, you can be proactive with just two straightforward documents that will help set your mind at ease for the future – a financial Power of Attorney and Advance Healthcare Directive (medical POA and Living Will).

Once you are named as Agent in these two documents, this will allow you to handle any necessary financial or medical situations needed on behalf of your adult child. You will be able to continue to protect your children with confidence as they navigate the many unexpected situations of life.

WHO

The **Principal** is the person granting the powers to be used.

The **Agent** is the person being granted powers to act on the Principal's behalf.

Powers can be allocated to more than one person, either acting together (both signatures required), or separately (only one or the other signature required).

When setting up Powers of Attorney and the Advance Healthcare Directive once your child turns 18, your adult child will be the Principal in this situation, and can name one or more Agents – which could include you as parents, or older siblings or other people of trust. Those individuals, as Agents, can access financial information and make financial decisions on behalf of your adult child. Such decisions could involve matters like paying tuition, room and board, rent, or even extend to medical bills.

WHAT

What happens if your 18-year-old child falls ill or becomes incapacitated? Someone must step in to make financial and medical decisions. Petitioning the court for guardianship becomes necessary if your child has not executed a Power of Attorney giving someone authority to act financially, or a Healthcare Power of Attorney giving someone authority to make medical decisions.

Though it might be the last thing on you or your child's mind, these basic elements of estate planning are important. Although it can be painful to think about, accidents can happen. It's likely that you or your child have seen it occur to friends already.

If your child is injured, someone needs the authority to make medical decisions and to work with insurance companies. Financial and medical POAs are required paperwork, even if you are already paying bills or your health insurance is responsible for the coverage of your adult child.

Sometimes colleges or other institutions will provide paperwork such as a consent form that your child can sign, granting information to you, but these are usually only good for one school year. These forms are often presented during an orientation prior to the first year, but are never updated or discussed after that. So if an issue arises in year two or three, the paperwork that could once be of assistance may no longer be valid.

In contrast, the financial and medical POA do not have an expiration date. Frequently these documents can remain valid and in place for years. In my experience, I often see them updated when a young adult gets married, naming the new spouse as an Agent in addition to, or instead of, parents.

In the absence of proper paperwork, you will be denied access to information when you need it most, and medical and financial providers will neither listen to you nor respect your decisions, even when those decisions are in the best interests of your child.

"When our son Jackson was taken to the hospital by ambulance from college, they would not tell us where he was sent, and the hospital would not call. We could not find him when he had his brain tumor. I had no idea where he was! It was a nightmare.

Even if you signed all the emergency contacts paperwork for college, it will not help you if your child is not able to reach you!"
—*DEANNA KELLY*

WHEN

When your child turns 18, make sure the right documents are in place, namely a Power of Attorney and Advance Healthcare Directive.

In these documents, you are recognized, legally, as an Agent for your child, which enables you to access needed information and to make important decisions in their best interests. These documents give you back the power, if needed, to help your child.

Let's face it, even at age 18, all children have much to learn and often still need help from a parent. The necessity can be even greater if your child will be living away from home. Can you remember some of the decisions you made when you were 18 years old?

WHY

The laws that once protected your child from prying outsiders, like HIPAA and the Family Educational Rights and Privacy Act (FERPA), now block your access to information. While "family" is in the name of FERPA, parents are *not* automatically allowed access to a child's educational records after their child turns 18. Accordingly, a parent could be faced with a challenging situation and the inability to obtain information.

Ryan Service Manzo

Director of Enrollment Services, Penn State York

"In the end, your role as a parent is going to be what you and your student choose for it to be. There's the emotional support side, and then there's the administrative financial side. You need to have a talk to establish an understanding so you can be supportive of each other and your choices.

FERPA really dictates a lot of what we at the university can share to parents and families. It's a federal law that protects the privacy of student records... grades, course listings, schedule, disciplinary records, financial records. We can't just release that information if a parent calls. There are ways for a student to grant access to certain aspects of their educational records. At Penn State we do have a process for that which we go through during orientation, but the student would need to take the initiative to grant access."

Here is an example:

A young girl graduates from high school, having done very well. She elects to continue her education at a university out of state. With financial and other assistance from her parents, she applies, is accepted, and moves to that university, which is located over ten hours away by car. Her freshman year begins, and the outlook is promising. However, the rigors of school and the distance from home become challenging.

The young girl encounters difficulties and suffers a nervous breakdown. Her parents, a few states away, want to provide assistance. They place calls and send emails seeking information since their daughter is not communicating with them. Unfortunately, because the issue is medical, care providers are unable to provide information because of HIPAA rules. Likewise, university officials are precluded from sharing because of their daughter's privacy rights under FERPA.

How could this dilemma have been avoided? Many institutions of higher learning, like Penn State, now allow students to sign documentation granting parents access to financial and other information. It is commonly discussed among a myriad of other topics during orientation. Such paperwork needs to be carefully reviewed, signed, and kept up to date.

A more enabling solution, which is not dependent on the university, is for your child to sign a Power of Attorney in favor of you as the parent. Such a POA allows parents access to records, is effective until revoked, and can transcend from one school year to the next.

Super Savvy Tip: To best protect your child and empower you to act quickly if needed, submit an original of this document to the university and request written confirmation of the institution's receipt and acknowledgment of its authority.

Another example:

Your adult child is driving home. A distracted driver in another car – focused on texting rather than the road – plows into your child. While the airbags deploy, injuries nonetheless follow. You might find your child in the hospital, unconscious. To the extent that a Healthcare POA has been put into effect, you can obtain information and make medical decisions for your child if needed.

While those two documents are often critical to have, sometimes young adults desire to create a Will to voice their wishes. Who gets their assets? Who serves as Executor? Do they want to dictate burial and funeral decisions, or allow another to make them? Documenting these decisions becomes especially important if the child's parents are no longer married. Without a Will, each parent has an equal right to control the estate, which can lead to avoidable conflict. Most young adults don't do Wills until they become married or have a child.

If your child becomes incapacitated, a durable general Power of Attorney appoints an Agent (or Agents) who will manage their assets. In a medical Power of Attorney and Living Will, your child chooses the person who will make medical decisions. If your child is ever unable to make decisions, the Agent steps in. This person selects doctors and authorizes or refuses treatment.

Accidents are the leading cause of death for young adults, and a quarter of a million Americans between the ages of 18 and 25 are hospitalized with non-lethal injuries each year. Can you imagine being unable to help or to make decisions for your child? It could happen if you fail to plan.

How

POA

As we've seen in Chapter Three, the Power of Attorney (POA) document allows an individual (known as the Principal) to name one or more Agents to access financial information and make financial decisions on their behalf.

A POA must be drafted under the laws of the state that the child calls home, but will be recognized as valid in other states and by institutions such as universities or colleges.

ADVANCE HEALTHCARE DIRECTIVE

As we saw in Chapter Four, an Advance Healthcare Directive also provides the ability for your adult child, in this case known as the Principal, the ability to appoint an Agent or Agents. Those Agents are allowed to access medical information and make medical decisions on behalf of your adult child if your child is unable to do so.

The Advance Healthcare Directive becomes crucial if your child becomes unconscious due to a physical injury, or becomes incapable of making such decisions personally because of a challenge with short-term stress or mental instability. This document can also be used if your child wants to be an organ donor. Again, such a document should be prepared in accordance with State law.

To take the next step, you should talk to your child about the importance of these documents and the benefit of putting them in place, so you can assist them if necessary. The process of preparing and executing the documents is not time-consuming.

You and your child may be fortunate enough to never have need to use them, but they are certainly a worthwhile investment. If they should become necessary and they provide assistance, they are priceless.

You never want to be in a situation where you are not empowered to help your children.

The financial cost associated with the creation of these documents is quite low compared to the devastating effects of not having a plan in place when needed. Often this planning is undertaken when a parent or grandparent offers to pay the legal fees.

Estate planning is often a focus for parents of young children or the elderly. However, all of us can find ourselves in situations where we need another to look after our best interests.

Utilization of a POA (and Healthcare POA) is a way to ensure that you can provide support to and receive support from your loved ones.

CAUTIONARY TALE
What no parent should have to face...

A friend's son was under stress at college. In fact, he admitted to his roommates that he might take his own life. The roommates reported the matter to campus security, and security personnel spoke with the young man. But they determined that he seemed okay. They did nothing further.

Hours later, the young man committed suicide. The world lost a kind, intelligent young adult who had so much potential.

You know what? The young man's parents received no notification from the college or anyone else that their son threatened to take his own life. They were denied the opportunity to talk with him and to try to understand what he was thinking. They were not empowered to help. Furthermore, they had no legal rights and no information.

There should have been the opportunity to prevent this ultimate tragedy.

Scott Simonds
Director of Student Affairs, Penn State York

"When extenuating circumstances happen, how do we mitigate that so the student can continue to move forward? When students are in difficulty, my team and I work with them to identify the need and see what we can do to deploy university resources so the student or family can be successful. That's the nice part about being part of a large university. We can often bring resources to bear and leverage those opportunities.

I think it's wise to have these documents and let the folks at your child's institution know. For example, if your student is going to see

---

someone in the counseling center for ongoing support, make sure those individuals know these documents are in place so you have the opportunity to weigh in on decisions that are really important.

I can recall situations where, because of extreme intoxication, a student was in a life-threatening situation. The parents were hours and hours away by car. It can make communication very challenging, particularly when divorce may be a situation. It's not always clear to the college who is the responsible parent. These documents provide clarity.

I love when parents come to our open houses and parent orientations. The more you know, the more you can help your student. Arm yourself with knowledge. Get to know the resources and get to know the institution. Don't be afraid to call and say, 'I'm concerned about my student...' We're always happy to work with parents. Don't be afraid to pick up the phone. But also let your student handle his or her own business. If you have questions, by all means, include your student as part of the conversation so we can have a full-fledged conversation with all information on the table."

My Invitation to You and Your Child

I have been practicing law for 27 years. I have drafted thousands of estate planning documents, for individuals as young as 18 and well into their 90s. I would be happy to talk with you about your family situation, to determine what documents might be necessary or appropriate to protect your interests and those of other family members too.

Contact me at **jrehmeyer@cgalaw.com** to talk about how we can begin this important planning process and complete it effectively and efficiently.

11

LIFE INSURANCE

The primary purpose of life insurance is to protect your spouse and children from financial loss in the event of your untimely death. Life insurance can provide financial security to your loved ones, allowing them to pay off debts, cover living expenses, and even pay medical costs related to your end-of-life care. Life insurance funds can also help cover final expenses like burial or cremation.

A life insurance policy can provide cash when your loved ones need it most, as typical policies pay out immediately upon your death with a lump-sum cash distribution which is generally not subject to federal income tax.

The payout of your life insurance policy goes to the recipient that you identify – the beneficiary – within the contract. Life insurance proceeds do not necessarily flow through the estate, nor are they subject to directives in a Will.

You need to be mindful and certain that the beneficiary designations and the balance of your estate plan coordinate. For example, if you name your children as a beneficiary, or contingent beneficiary, in a life insurance policy, and you die, then that money will go to them directly. If they're under 18, it would be held only until their 18th birthday. Alternately, if you utilize a family Trust in your Will to hold assets for your children, then that Trust should be named as the beneficiary under the life insurance policy instead of the children themselves.

What all of these policies have in common is that they are a legal agreement between you and the insurer. In exchange for your routine payments called "premiums," which can be paid monthly or annually, the policy offers a "death benefit amount" that is agreed upon at the beginning of coverage and will be paid out in the case of your death.

Some life insurance policies with larger death benefits require a medical examination before enrollment. During such an exam, the insurer collects information like your height, weight, and blood pressure. Additionally it uses blood and urine tests to screen for health conditions like high cholesterol and drug or nicotine use. It is not uncommon for smokers to be charged higher insurance premiums because of the higher likelihood of smoking-related illness and death.

Premiums can be a fixed amount for the life of the policy, or may vary over time based on your current age and health status. In all cases, you must continue to pay these premiums on time to maintain life insurance coverage. Failure to keep up with payments for any reason can result in premature termination of the policy. Any lapse in payment could potentially result in the insurance company denying a claim if you die while a premium balance remains unpaid.

Life insurance is an important estate planning tool and can be a valuable way to protect your family. If you die early, it ensures your ability to still pass an inheritance to loved ones. Conversely, if you live a long or medically extended life, it provides the assurance of an inheritance even though you depleted your savings.

HOW MUCH COVERAGE?
You should always consult a licensed insurance agent to determine the best amount of coverage and the wisest policy type based on your individual circumstances. However, you might benefit from considering the most common uses families have for life insurance death benefits.

Income replacement is one possibility. If you are your family's primary earner, consider the expenses your salary typically covers in the course of the year.

Many families use life insurance to pay off a mortgage, thereby eliminating one of the largest and most common monthly recurring household expenses.

For families with one or more young children, the cost of childcare can represent a significant ongoing outlay. Likewise, families with one or more children approaching college age can face a time of enormous need for funds to cover tuition and housing expenses.

If someone in your household requires routine healthcare or long-term care, that could also present a financial obstacle, especially if you were the one whose job covered the cost of medical or long-term care insurance at the time of your death.

Some families benefit from peace of mind, knowing that life insurance funds would be available to alleviate household debt at the time of your death. In addition to a mortgage, this might include things like credit card debt, a home equity loan, auto loans, and student loans.

If you own a business or participate in a family business, life insurance could be a way to alleviate the financial burden for the company to continue in your absence. Definitely consult a licensed insurance broker and your attorney to ensure the policy is written and the beneficiary or beneficiaries are named in such a way as to carry out your wishes.

TYPES OF COVERAGE
The two main types of life insurance policies are:

- Term life
- Whole life

TERM LIFE

Term life insurance is usually the easiest to acquire and has the cheapest premiums. It can provide a financial safety net for your loved ones in the event of your death.

A term policy is negotiated for a set length of time, or "term," during which you routinely pay a premium in exchange for a fixed death benefit amount. If you die during the period of coverage, then the amount of your policy is paid to the beneficiary designated within the policy. If you survive through the policy's end date, the money remains with the insurer and the policy lapses.

Term life insurance varies between 10 to 30 years in coverage. It often provides a higher death benefit for a lower premium than other types of coverage, but the downside is that if you outlive your policy, there is no cash value or refund of your policy premiums.

This kind of insurance policy is frequently taken out prior to a person's highest-earning years, because it's less expensive. Despite this lower cost, it can generate funds earmarked to take care of substantial financial obligations like a mortgage and college education.

Term life insurance is also sometimes used to provide financial security and stability for business partners or key executives in a company, in the event of someone's death that could cause financial loss to the company.

WHOLE LIFE

Whole life insurance is the most common because of its simplicity and longer duration. As with term life, you and the insurer contract for a specific dollar amount of death benefit in exchange for payment of a monthly or annual premium. The difference is that *whole life* policies extend through your whole life, rather than just a set term like 10 or 20 or 30 years.

Another difference is that the premiums paid for a whole life policy typically accumulate a cash value which earns interest over time, at a fixed rate set by the insurer. Premiums remain the same for the lifetime of the policy, and are set based on the age and health of the insured at the time the insurance commences.

The way whole life works is that a portion of your premiums go to cover the cost of maintenance of the policy, and the rest accrues cash value in your account.

For some, this represents a low-risk investment and is a way to begin or encourage a lifelong savings habit.

One notable difference between term and whole life is that with a whole life policy, your cash value earns interest over time, and after you've accumulated enough cash value, you can either borrow or withdraw money from this account.

The obvious benefits of whole life are the cash value that you retain and the longer duration of coverage. The downside, however, is that whole life policies are more costly and complex. There are often certain medical exclusions and whole life is more expensive than term life for a death benefit of an equivalent amount.

In addition to these two main types of life insurance policies, there are three common variations:

- Universal life

- Variable life

- Final expenses

UNIVERSAL LIFE

Universal life insurance provides flexibility, as it allows you to increase or decrease premiums based on your policy's current cash value. Essentially, once your policy accrues a certain cash value, you can use that to offset the payment of premiums as desired.

This type of coverage can be more expensive, however, than a standard whole life policy, especially as the basic premium amounts increase with your age.

VARIABLE LIFE

Variable life insurance allows you to invest the money from your cash value in various funds offered by the insurance company, often including mutual funds.

These policies come with a guaranteed death benefit, however, your cash value is not guaranteed at a fixed rate of interest. Whatever fund you choose to invest your cash benefit in determines the earnings that money will realize.

It is possible that your cash value with a variable life policy could outperform a whole life policy with a similar cash value, but you could also lose money if the fund performs poorly in market conditions.

FINAL EXPENSES

Final expense insurance, also known as burial insurance, provides a relatively small death benefit to help offset the cost of end-of-life expenses.

There is typically no medical exam and little to no waiting period before coverage begins, but the policy often comes at a higher premium for lower coverage amounts.

This type of life insurance policy is often best for seniors and those with serious health conditions who have trouble qualifying for traditional coverage.

SURVIVORSHIP/JOINT LIFE

Another variation is survivorship life insurance, also known as joint life insurance, which pays out one of two ways.

First-to-die policies pay the death benefit to the surviving spouse (or other beneficiary, as it is not necessary for both policy holders to be married to each other) upon the death of the first policy holder.

Survivorship, or second-to-die, policies pay out upon the death of both policy holders. Typically less expensive than two separate permanent policies, it can be especially helpful if you want to leave an inheritance for heirs, permanently dependent children, or even a charity.

If either you or your partner has difficulty qualifying for coverage through a standard life insurance policy due to age or medical condition, joint life might be a viable alternative as both policy owners will be factored in to your eligibility rather than just one.

One downside of a joint life policy is that it can be difficult to update coverage in the event of divorce or other significant life change. In instances like this, you may want to consider inquiring about the possibility of splitting the coverage.

Another weakness is that for second-to-die policies, the second policyholder cannot be a beneficiary, as that person must also pass before a death benefit is paid out.

IRREVOCABLE LIFE INSURANCE TRUST

Because life insurance is often a key component of estate planning, it is helpful to understand a possibility available to you that allow the proceeds of a life insurance policy to be excluded from your estate, thereby removing them for federal estate tax purposes, which may provide substantial tax savings upon your death.

An Irrevocable Life Insurance Trust (ILIT) is a Trust that is created with the sole purpose of owning an insurance policy on the Settlor's life. The Trust is named as the beneficiary of the policy.

When you die and your life insurance policy is owned by a properly funded and administered ILIT, the death benefits are not included in your estate because the Trust, rather than you, is the owner and beneficiary.

One common use of an ILIT is to provide liquidity for the payment of estate tax liabilities when loved ones may not otherwise have the cash to pay.

Upon your death, life insurance proceeds are typically handled one of two ways. They may be transferred to the ILIT and held, or distributed to the Trust beneficiaries outright. Or they may be used by a Trustee to purchase assets from the estate to enable the payment of estate taxes without having to liquidate estate assets to do so. This is typically done when an estate does not have enough liquidity to pay estate taxes by the due date, or when the deceased does not want assets to be sold upon death, preferring they be transferred in kind to beneficiaries.

While an ILIT can offer tremendous benefits, consider that a Trust of this type requires more documentation and creates administrative burdens when dealing with the life insurance policy. As with all Trusts, the upfront work and expense is completely wasted if assets are not properly titled and transferred to the Trust.

CAUTIONARY TALE

When it comes to insurance, it's important to be mindful of the purpose for which you want to obtain it, rather than simply have it sold to you. For example, I bought a term policy when my children were young. Now that my children have graduated college, and the term policy has ended, I am not seeking to replace this policy with another because its purpose was served. Namely, being in place to protect my family if I died while the children were young.

YOU MEAN I CAN SELL MY LIFE INSURANCE?

Some policyholders find that over time their life insurance policy is no longer needed, or they can no longer afford the premiums. There is currently an "aftermarket" for life insurance policies of those aged 65 and older. Some third-party companies, fueled by investors, will purchase your life insurance policy from you – paying your premiums until death, and then receiving the entirety of the death benefits.

After studying actuarial tables, these investors determine what percentage of your death benefit amount they are willing to pay. According to the Life Insurance Settlement Association, the average life settlement is 20 percent of the face value of your coverage.[8]

For example, if you have $500,000 worth of coverage, after an application and appraisal process, a licensed buyer or broker might purchase your policy for $100,000. Once you accept the offer, a set of documents is prepared, and a contract and disclosure forms are sent to you for signature. The buyer would then become responsible for premium payments, but would

---

[8] http://lisa.org

also be the sole beneficiary of your insurance benefits upon your death.

While this practice is completely legal as of the writing of this book, you should certainly consider the depth of impact of such a decision upon your broader estate planning.

Furthermore, the income gained from the sale of your policy is typically taxable and may disqualify you from receiving Medicaid or other financial assistance programs.

R. Gregory Nicholas, CIC, FSCP, LUTCF
Allstate Insurance

"You buy life insurance for the family left behind, not for yourself. Your estate plan and life insurance work together. You want to make sure that you have enough life insurance to cover all the debt you have, and then to provide an income stream for the family left behind. That needs to take into consideration college funding and all the stuff that is part of living. Make sure everyone knows who's been picked [to handle your estate] and why. Have conversations with those key family members.

Term insurance is what I recommend most for young families. They can buy the most amount of insurance to cover their need, and it's cost effective as they move through life. The whole life policy is permanent. It can't be changed once you set the premium. It goes forward and it's very consistent. Universal life came out of the idea of a hybrid policy. It gives you the ability to change the premium. You can put in lump sums. You can stop paying the premium. You can say, 'I want it to end at a certain date.' It gives the customer a lot more options.

We do planning every two to three years to update. If you have a life event, we need to get together and see how that affects your plans."

12
EMPLOYEE BENEFITS

Depending on where you work, you may receive employer-provided benefits in addition to your salary or hourly wages. The most common types of employee benefits are life insurance, disability insurance, a long-term care policy, and a retirement plan. These vary significantly depending on whether you are employed by a private company or by the state or federal government.

Remember not to take these benefits for granted and fail to adequately coordinate them with your estate planning goals.

EMPLOYER-PROVIDED
LIFE INSURANCE POLICY

An employer-provided life insurance policy is typically a group life insurance that offers a death benefit equivalent to your annual salary, or in some cases, two or three times your annual salary.

Depending on your debt, family size, and overall wishes, the death benefit can be insufficient for your needs, and really should only be considered supplemental in nature.

Identifying the appropriate amount of life insurance death benefit is particular to your wants and needs and should be discussed with a licensed insurance professional.

Most group life insurance policies are guaranteed issue, meaning that you will be eligible regardless of your health and medical history. If you find yourself leaving your current employer (and benefits), most group life insurance policies will not transfer with you, and you must seek an individual policy. Unfortunately, individual life insurance policies are not guaranteed issue, and your individual age and medical condition will impact your premium costs and even insurability.

Insurance of this type presents another opportunity to coordinate how assets will be left to your loved ones. For example, if this money is going to a spouse, that person can be named as the beneficiary. If the proceeds are going to your children, especially if they are minors, you would want to pass assets through your Will, which hopefully establishes a Trust that can receive and hold assets for the benefit of your children over time, under the watch of a Trustee.

Insurance proceeds, whether or not they flow through probate, are not subject to inheritance tax.

EMPLOYER-PROVIDED
DISABILITY INSURANCE

A disability can be just as challenging for a family as a death. When you become disabled, not only will you and your loved ones have to deal with legal and financial issues, but also someone will need to take care of you.

In-home healthcare comes with its own costs and ramifications, depending on the quality and level of care, and rehabilitation facilities can be shockingly expensive.

Medicare and many health insurances cease payment for daily care after a period of 90 days. While government aid programs are available, most of these require you to exhaust your own assets first.

If you are among the 35 percent[9] of employees in the U.S. whose employer sponsors disability insurance, you should still be aware that these policies usually do not cover 100 percent of your lost income. Most replace at the rate of around 60 percent.

---

[9] According to U.S. Bancorp Investments, February 9, 2023.

These employer-sponsored plans typically have an elimination period of 30 days to 2 years, during which you must wait to begin collecting benefits.

An additional worry is that if your coverage is paid with pre-tax dollars, any benefits you receive will be taxable.

According to the Council for Disability Awareness, one in four adults will become disabled before retirement age.[10] The average long-term disability claim lasts nearly 3 years. Leading causes are car accidents, cancer, and heart attack and stroke, but issues resulting from back injuries and even diabetes can cause an inability to work. Mental decline such as dementia or Alzheimer's can be completely incapacitating.

SHORT-TERM DISABILITY POLICIES

Short-term disability insurance typically covers in the event of illness or injury for a period of 3 to 6 months.

As of 2023, only five U.S. states require employers to provide such policies: California, Hawaii, New Jersey, New York, and Rhode Island.

In Pennsylvania, the Family and Medical Leave Act (FMLA) offers eligible employees access to paid medical, caregiving, parental, and deployment leave.

LONG-TERM DISABILITY POLICIES

Virtually all long-term disability insurance has a waiting period of 3 to 6 months before benefits begin. This is where the overlap of short-term and long-term disability coverage is helpful.

Employer-provided plans typically only offer coverage to full-time employees. Each company's definition of "full-time" will vary, but ranges from at least 30 to 35 hours per week.

---

[10] https://disabilitycanhappen.org/

Be aware that many long-term disability policies have exclusions for pre-existing conditions, typically a period of 90 to 180 days from the date when coverage begins.

The length of coverage can last through retirement age, but depending on the illness or injury, benefits may cap out at 24 months. Additionally, many policies require that you also submit for Social Security Disability insurance benefits, which would offset the benefit amount required to be paid by the main policy itself.

If you have medical issues or become disabled, you may want to revisit the Advance Healthcare Directive which would appoint an Agent for medical decisions and express your wishes in regard to healthcare.

LONG-TERM CARE POLICIES

Employers are unlikely to provide any type of long-term care insurance, but this should be an option to consider that would provide financial security in the event you can no longer perform the most basic of day to day activities: bathing, dressing, feeding yourself, getting from a bed to a chair, and using the toilet. If you develop cognitive impairment, long-term care insurance can also kick in.

In Pennsylvania, coverage provides for services in your home, in a care facility, or a combination of both. This might take the form of skilled nursing care, intermediate care, custodial care, adult day care, or hospice care.

According to the Pennsylvania Insurance Department's website, about two-thirds of us will eventually require some form of long-term care. In addition to home health or community care services, benefits can also be used to cover costs for meal preparation, household tasks, and even grocery shopping.[11]

The 2023 Genworth Cost of Care Study reported that the annual cost of a semi-private nursing home room in Pennsylvania in 2021 was about $124,800. The cost of a one-bedroom assisted living facility was about $49,200. The cost of a home health aid was about $59,500. These costs must be paid by the policyholder during the policy's elimination period (typically, the first 90 days of care). The policyholder will also be liable for costs that exceed the policy's daily or monthly payment limit.[12]

While long-term care insurance can be extremely valuable, it can also be very costly. If you obtain it, you should consider what present and future premiums will be. You should also be mindful of the coverage that you will receive. It's not uncommon for premiums to increase substantially, which causes individuals to terminate the policies. It's also not uncommon for individuals to expect to receive more benefits than they actually get.

In the event that you die without needing long-term care, the premiums you have paid are lost without benefit. Consider such policies as "use it or lose it."

If you decide to use long-term care insurance to ensure future financial security, this is another part of your plan that needs to be carefully considered both initially and over time to ensure the benefits are maximized.

HEALTH FLEXIBLE SPENDING AND SAVINGS ACCOUNTS
A health savings account (HSA) is like a savings account that can be used only for medical expenses. They can offer tax

---

[11] https://www.insurance.pa.gov/Coverage/Pages/Long-Term-Care-for-Seniors.aspx

[12] https://www.genworth.com/aging-and-you/finances/cost-of-care.html

advantages, as contributions to an HSA are made using pre-tax dollars, allowing you to pay less income tax for the year.

Be cautious, however, as withdrawing funds from an HSA for non-qualified expenses before you turn 65 can result in income taxes plus a 20 percent penalty.

A flexible spending account (FSA) allows you to deposit money pre-tax which can be used to pay for certain out-of-pocket healthcare costs, like deductibles, copayments, coinsurance, and prescription medications. They can also be used to pay for medical equipment like crutches or wheelchairs, or supplies like bandages and diagnostic devices.

As an employee, you submit a claim to the FSA through your employer with proof of the medical expense along with a statement indicating that the cost has not been covered by insurance. The costs are then reimbursed through the FSA.

Check with your employer, as FSAs have dollar-amount limitations as to how much may be saved and used annually. As of 2023, that amount is $3,050 per year per employer.

Chris Rice, CFP, CPA/PFS
E.K. McConkey Insurance & Benefits

"A health flexible spending account (FSA) and a health savings account (HSA) sound very similar but are quite different. Each of them allow you to contribute to an account pre-tax, however, with an HSA, you must be enrolled in a qualified high-deductible plan to even participate. With an FSA, you can participate in almost any plan as long as the FSA is available through your employer and you're not also contributing to an HSA, because you can't contribute to both at the same time.

Another difference between HSAs and FSA is with an HSA you can actually pay for current year, prior year, or future year expenses, so if you put money away today, and if you have a payment plan on a huge bill you had two years ago, you can use that fund right now, or you can roll it over to future years. With an FSA, it's use it or lose it the same year.

The HSA is actually the most efficient investment account that there is because it's tax-free into the account and it's tax-free out of the account. There's no other account that can be both tax-free in and tax-free out.

Voluntary benefits are a part of your package that you have the option of whether you want to participate. One particular situation where this comes in handy is when someone is otherwise uninsurable, especially in cases of life insurance and disability insurance. A lot of voluntary benefits are issued on what is called a Guaranteed Standard Issue basis, so there's no underwriting involved. In other words, nobody's going to pull your medical records to see that maybe you have a debilitating condition. You're not going to have to do blood work or medical exams. This creates a different route to get protections for your family, especially if you have some unique circumstances. Make sure you're maximizing these voluntary benefits that a number of employers make available.

We recommend you review coverage every 5 years.

If you're an employer, investigate these options because they can be used to entice and retain employees. Conversely, if you're an employee looking at your options, it's not simply a matter of salary or vacation, but you really want to dive into the benefit options to see what your employer makes available to protect you and your family."

EMPLOYER-ISSUED STOCK OPTIONS

An employee stock option (ESO) is a form of equity compensation that can be granted to certain employees and company executives.

ESO grants typically come in the form of regular call options and give an employee the right to buy company stock at a specified price for a finite period of time.

The stock option will have a vesting schedule – the length of time which an employee must work for the company before eligibility – but may contribute substantial earnings over time, even if the stock option initially has little intrinsic value.

You should be aware that ESOs are taxed both at the time of exercise and when shares are sold on the open market.

Stocks received through such options are assets that should be addressed and distributed through your Will.

EMPLOYER-PROVIDED RETIREMENT PLAN

While employer-provided pension plans that offer a lifetime stream of revenue for vested retirees were quite common for previous generations, there may still be a retirement plan to which you can contribute a pre-tax portion of your salary. In many instances, the employer will match your contributions, typically up to 3 percent of your wages.

One of the most common retirement plans is the 401K, but there are other options like the 403 B, SEP, 457, Thrift Savings Plan, and the simple IRA.

Retirement plans are different than group life insurance policies because you can transfer the balance of your retirement plan when you change employers. In some cases, your employers' contributions have not "vested," and your employer will retain their contributions to your plan because you have not worked for the company for a sufficient time.

Retirement plans allow for beneficiary designations. Accordingly, you will need to coordinate these designations with other aspects of your estate plan. If you would prefer your retirement funds to flow to your children, especially if they are minors, then consider either naming your Will (or a Trust that flows through the Will) as the beneficiary. For example, a beneficiary designation intended to funnel assets for children to a Trust might read: "To the Family Trust in my Last Will and Testament dated [month, day, date]..."

Remember that taxable assets don't change whether or not they go through probate. Retirement plan monies flowing outside of probate are still subject to inheritance tax.

EMPLOYEE BENEFITS AND YOUR ESTATE PLAN

Depending on the type of estate plan you have, the steps to coordinate your employer-provided benefits will differ, though typically life insurance death benefits and retirement plans pay out directly to designated beneficiaries, often circumventing the probate process.

Unfortunately, naming a person as a direct beneficiary doesn't always provide protections or assurances for use of the funds. For instance, if an immature 18-year-old beneficiary is designated, the funds will proceed to them outside of probate or any Trust that could be managed to their benefit by a Trustee until that person is deemed to be able to make prudent financial decisions for themselves. Similarly, if a beneficiary received assets directly from employer-provided benefits and then commingled those assets with their spouse, a divorce could result in the loss of the inherited assets.

When a Revocable Living Trust is used, the Trust can be named as a beneficiary of life insurance as well as retirement accounts. This can impact taxes due, and can also shield any beneficiary who is receiving needs-based government benefits like SSI or Medicaid from disqualification.

As with all estate planning needs, there are many dynamics involved in evaluating the most efficient and effective manner of passing assets at death. If you have specific questions regarding your options for employer-related benefits, consider consulting with an insurance professional or the company's human resources officer.

13

CHOOSING AN ATTORNEY
& DEMYSTIFYING FEES

Sometimes, the most challenging part of the estate planning process is overcoming procrastination to schedule an initial consultation. After selecting a lawyer and arranging a visit, you can make the initial meeting more productive by providing in advance, or bringing with you, the following information:

- A list of what you own. If you own it with somebody else, also bring the name of that person, and how you own it;

- A list of your intended beneficiaries, with their full names, ages, and addresses (if they do not live with you);

- A short list of individuals upon whom you could rely, while you are alive, or after you pass, who could serve as an Executor, Agent, Trustee and/or Guardian (if applicable);

- A list of all the questions that you have about estate planning.

This will enable your attorney to spend more time developing a plan and less time writing down basic information.

There are many areas of law. Not all lawyers have the knowledge, skill, judgment, or experience to plan your estate properly to preserve your assets and protect your family. Be sure to select an attorney who focuses on Estate Planning.

You will also benefit by selecting a lawyer who has access to other professionals and research options for circumstances that crop up or are unique to you and your situation or assets.

As with anything in life, it is always preferable to work with someone who wants to help you efficiently and effectively. This avoids both unnecessary administrative and legal costs.

QUALITIES TO LOOK FOR IN AN ESTATE LAWYER

Ultimately, it's most important to work with a lawyer you trust and who is responsive to you. Nothing is more essential in your attorney/client relationship.

The right estate attorney is one who will answer all your questions. You cannot make the best decisions if you have doubts or your questions remain unanswered. This should be a base level of service. Anything else is unacceptable.

You also want a lawyer who will return your phone calls promptly and answer emails in a timely manner. Never retain a lawyer who fails to respond to your needs. In fact many clients have come to me over the years, specifically because other attorneys were unresponsive.

While I prefer to communicate by phone, email, or letter, I will nonetheless respond to text messages, especially when something important has arisen.

Ideally, work with an attorney who has roots in your community. That person will have an established reputation and is more likely to provide excellent service. That person should also be around to continue serving your needs for years to come. Additionally, when working with an attorney who is part of a law firm, that relationship creates more depth for a wider provision of legal services.

5 Of course, you will want an attorney whose fees are fair. If the fee is too low, it is likely something is being left out. Too high, and they may be overcharging you. Many will provide a free initial phone call, or a consultation at a nominal fee. Use this time to get to know the person so you can make a more informed decision of whether to hire that lawyer.

After reading this book, you will likely have found one or more chapters that are specific to your needs. Make a short list of questions to talk about in this consultation, such as: "How can I reduce inheritance taxes?" or "What's the most savvy way to leave money for my child or grandchild's education?"

FEE STRUCTURES

How can you decide what attorney fees are fair and reasonable? There are four main fee structures in most legal work:

- Hourly

- Flat fee

- Recovery-based, or contingent fees (often comes into play for personal injury cases)

- Percentage-based

FIXED HOURLY RATE

Most transactional work, like developing a contract or completing the purchase of a business, is based on the time involved, billed at an hourly rate. Every lawyer has a fixed hourly rate.

When an attorney bills on an hourly basis, they track in increments of an hour – sometimes as precise as tenths of an hour. There is software that helps track the time for accuracy.

Don't let a stiff hourly rate scare you though, as experienced attorneys are often far more efficient than someone who bills at a lower rate but is less experienced in the area of the law you need. For example, you might be better served to pay $350 per hour to someone who could complete the work exceptionally well than to pay $200 per hour to someone who will take twice as long and leave devastating gaps in your legal documentation.

Sometimes estate planning is done on an hourly basis, and other times it is offered at a flat fee.

FLAT FEE

Flat fees are typically utilized by lawyers when they have a high degree of certainty about the scope of work involved before they even begin. For example, the formation of a limited liability company or filing a basic bankruptcy are legal services that can often be obtained for a flat fee.

Attorneys offering estate planning at a fixed fee will need to understand your specific situation before quoting a dollar amount. The amount of work and number of documents will vary, as you've seen from the preceding chapters. However, most estate planning attorneys will feel comfortable quoting a ballpark figure for spouses with two children, including the essential documents of a Will (with a Trust for Minor Children), Powers of Attorney, and Healthcare Powers of Attorney. Legal services for estate planning under these circumstances, in my experience, typically cost less than a monthly mortgage payment, or perhaps even rent in your area.

Perhaps a helpful way to place attorney fees into perspective is to consider the fee in light of the importance of the matter or the dollars involved. For most people, there is a vast difference between protecting a replaceable item of negligible value versus ensuring the protection of a multimillion-dollar estate and loved ones.

RECOVERY-BASED OR CONTINGENCY FEES

Recovery-based or contingency fees are those you often hear about in the advertisements for personal injury attorneys. *"We don't get paid unless you get paid."* While there is no up-front financial outlay for the client, these attorneys will evaluate your case as to its potential recovery value, knowing that these attorneys will claim anywhere from 25 to 40 percent of what they do in fact recover for their client. Similarly, worker's compensation legal services are often performed on a contingent fee basis. This is generally not relevant in estate planning.

PERCENTAGE-BASED

In 1983, the *Johnson Estate* case established a percentage-based form of fee structure for estate administration. Specifically, the attorney's fees will be a small percentage of the value and type of assets within the estate. Such percentages typically range from 1 to 5 percent. For example, the percentage is low on a bank account, but when real estate is involved, the percentage increases. Please remember that real estate presents a great deal more work for the attorney who will likely review the Agreement of Sale, interact with the seller and buyer, provide deed research and transfer, and attend settlement.

A judge in Montgomery County, Pennsylvania, supported the *Johnson* scale, saying that using hours as a sole method for fixing compensation "penalizes the efficient attorney."

An increasing number of clients actually prefer the *Johnson* scale or percentage-based attorney fee arrangement so they understand total costs at the outset rather than risking a bill with runaway hours. These percentages are typically less than people pay in other circumstances, like selling a house with a real estate agent, as those are usually 6 to 7 percent.

If your lawyer suggests the *Johnson* scale and your assets are primarily cash-based, you may want to discuss whether the lawyer is willing to reduce the applicable percentages. Depending upon your circumstances, it may be possible to negotiate an hourly agreement with a cap that is often percentage-based.

Sometimes attorneys will serve as both Executor (if needed) as well as the attorney of record. There is efficiency if the attorney serves as both. However, the attorney should not be allowed to double dip, collecting both full attorney fees as well as an Executor's commission.

FAIR'S FAIR

Again you ask, how do you know what's *fair* and *reasonable*?

According to a 1968 court case, the following factors were established:

- The character of the services to be performed

- The difficulty of the problems involved

- The importance of litigation

- The amount of money or value of property in question

- The degree of responsibility incurred

- Whether there is a fund created to cover professional fees

- The standing of the attorney

- The ability of the client to pay

Fee structure can vary based upon the amount of work to be done and the complexity of that work. You should have some discussion with the attorney to establish expectations.

Estate planning fees often start at hundreds of dollars for a single individual, but can rise to thousands of dollars for complicated planning. Estate administration legal fees, however, typically start at thousands of dollars but can elevate to tens of thousands of dollars.

It is important to be mindful of attorney fees and how they will be determined. Recognize that professional assistance under certain circumstances is often imperative to protect your interests, avoid mistakes, and preserve the value of assets that pass to loved ones.

I have often been engaged to assist in fixing problems, and the fees are usually substantially more than they would have been to do it well initially.

I've been involved in many estates that could have benefitted from better, more effective estate planning on the front end. Similarly, I've been involved in several estates after administration commenced, to help fix problems which could have been avoided if my assistance had been sought earlier in the process.

While attorneys are not necessarily inexpensive, the failure to utilize them can often be very costly.

14
CONCLUSION

Ralph Waldo Emerson said, "Life is a journey, not a destination." At the time of my application to law school, despite being only 24 years old, I already accumulated mileage. With two years at the U.S. Naval Academy and an Economics degree from California State University, Long Beach, I had worked as a dishwasher, busboy, waiter, lifeguard, bartender, insurance salesman, and investment advisor. I came to know the joy of interacting with others and helping them.

As an attorney, I have enjoyed the opportunity to interact with real estate brokers, developers, lenders, and elected officials, seeing the results of my work in the community in which I live – substantial buildings, and even a professional baseball stadium.

Over time, my practice has transformed to one that is guiding and transactional. Estate planning became a focus early on and it has only grown. As life went on, I enjoyed a number of wonderful experiences – like the birth of my children – and suffered some devastating ones, too, including the divorces of friends and family and the deaths of loved ones.

I have come to realize that attorneys can either fix problems after they have happened, or try to prevent them in the first place. Preparing and preventing problems always seemed to be the better course of action, if it could be undertaken. My appreciation increased continually with regard to the importance of planning ahead and trying to be ready to deal with problems should they arise, rather than reacting to them after they arise.

Be mindful of key milestones that can indicate the need to undertake or revisit your estate planning documents.

- Marriage
- Birth of a child
- When a child turns 18
- Significant travel
- Birth of a grandchild
- Medical diagnosis or surgery
- Divorce

In addition, be mindful of your current situation and how your planning documents would apply to it. Consider family dynamics, like how your kids are doing financially, or whether your parents are experiencing difficulty in independently managing their affairs.

If you ask and answer the right questions, estate planning doesn't need to be that complicated. Many attorneys will be happy to "sell" you planning that may be more complicated or more expensive than you need. Always remember to be mindful of what services you need and why you're obtaining them.

Over the years, you have developed relationships with many people. Some of those are professionals upon whom you can rely. Those relationships can help you and others. For example, many of my current clients are either family or friends of previous clients. All professionals appreciate such referrals, but also remember that your friends and family will be even more appreciative when you can refer them to someone you know and trust.

The spread of the Coronavirus created substantial impacts across the globe. For some, it created turmoil when named Agents, Executors, Guardians, or Trustees became unable or unwilling to serve. Consider how widespread health concerns may affect your current or future estate planning needs.

As a final reminder, make sure that your original estate planning documents are at a known location, and your family can find them. And please, please, please have a conversation with those you wish to designate as Agent, Executor, Guardian, or Trustee, so you all feel confident about their ability to perform the necessary tasks in accordance with your wishes and best interests.

Ideally, these matters should be addressed and documents set in place before you become ill. Many of these documents can be prepared after telephone or email communication, and then be executed with minimal in-person contact.

It is my greatest hope that through the use of the information contained in this book, you feel empowered to take action now to protect yourself and your loved ones using at a minimum the four essential documents outlined in Chapter Two:

- Power of Attorney (POA)
- Advance Healthcare Directive
  (Medical POA and Living Will)
- Last Will and Testament
- Final Instruction Letter

You can approach estate planning in a S.M.A.R.T. and effective way by:

Setting goals
Making your documents accessible
Absolving your family of burdens
Relieving chaos and confusion
Taking care of family and loved ones

S.M.A.R.T. estate planning is not about being brainy, but rather about being efficient and effective. Ask the questions you need answered so you can more readily understand issues surrounding the protection of your family – especially around estate planning, which will make everything less complicated.

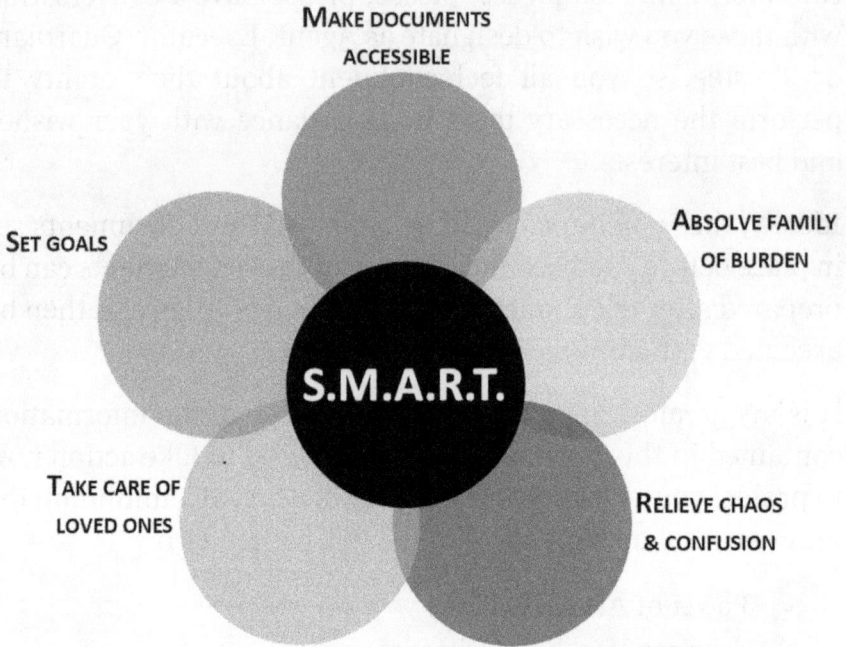

MAKE DOCUMENTS
ACCESSIBLE

ABSOLVE FAMILY
OF BURDEN

SET GOALS

S.M.A.R.T.

TAKE CARE OF
LOVED ONES

RELIEVE CHAOS
& CONFUSION

Ultimately, no plan is effective unless the essential documents have been completed and executed. Even the best estate plan, if not implemented, is no estate plan at all.

My goal is to help you get the information you need so you can overcome any hesitation or procrastination. We all want to feel the reassurance of having an estate plan that takes care of our best interests and is updated over time to continue best protecting and serving those we love most.

If you would like to discuss estate planning documents or have any questions, please contact me. There will not be any charge for a simple inquiry. And if you need something done, I will help you as promptly and efficiently as possible.

---

www.SMARTestateplanbook.com

I am excited that you made it to the final chapter of the book. If you find yourself ready to think further about your estate planning, and implement it now, I would be happy to help.

Visit **www.SMARTestateplanbook.com** and download the Goal Setting document and the Estate Planning Questionnaire. Identify the goals that are your priority and provide information that could be used to prepare estate planning documents.

COMPLIMENTARY CALL

Need a conversation to talk about next steps? I'd be happy to speak with you to see how I could be of assistance.

Please reach out to schedule your free initial consultation. (zoom or phone)

(717) 848-4900 (office)

jrehmeyer@cgalaw.com

If you live in a state beyond those within which I am licensed to practice, or you have an attorney of your own, I encourage you to seek local counsel and proceed promptly.

Appendix A

Goal Setting Document

This document can help you understand and prioritize what is most important to you. When doing estate planning, there are often trade-offs. You can't always achieve each and every goal. For example, some have to relinquish control or ownership of assets to achieve tax savings.

For downloadable and
printable documents visit:

www.SMARTestateplanbook.com

ᵀᴴᴱ S.M.A.R.T. ESTATE PLAN
Protecting You and Your Family

Goal Setting Document
Estate Plan Objectives

- ☐ Select the best people to look after my children, if I cannot.
- ☐ Select the most qualified people to oversee money that I leave for my children.
- ☐ Avoid selecting a representative who might be unwilling or unable to actively handle my estate
- ☐ Minimize inheritance taxes
- ☐ Avoid delays in handling my estate
- ☐ Avoid making my personal affairs public
- ☐ Avoid losing control of my assets to the Court
- ☐ Avoid ancillary administration in other states where I own property
- ☐ Avoid the payment of estate taxes on life insurance
- ☐ Avoid paying Federal estate taxes on assets with very high values
- ☐ Avoid the dangers of owning property that is not properly titled
- ☐ Avoid the unintentional disinheritance of my children
- ☐ Avoid quarrels and lawsuits among heirs over my assets
- ☐ Protect my minor children from the need for guardianship proceedings before the orphan's court
- ☐ Prevent anyone from changing my estate planning
- ☐ Prevent the need for guardianships or conservatorships
- ☐ Provide for me in the event of my physical or mental incapacity
- ☐ Reduce emotional stress for my spouse and family members
- ☐ Save hundreds, or maybe thousands of dollars, in court costs and fees
- ☐ Make sure that I don't become a burden to my children

Additional goals that are personal to your family's unique situations:

- ☐
- ☐
- ☐
- ☐

JEFFREY L. REHMEYER II

CGA Law Firm | 717-848-4900 (office) | 717-718-7115 (direct) | jrehmeyer@cgalaw.com

APPENDIX B

Estate Planning Questionnaire

This document helps you gather information that is necessary to complete effective planning. It also includes questions that have to be answered to protect your loved ones.

For downloadable and
printable documents visit:

www.SMARTestateplanbook.com

THE S.M.A.R.T. ESTATE PLAN
Protecting You and Your Family

Estate Planning Questionnaire

This information will assist you and trusted counsel to most efficiently create documents that will ensure your desires are carried out as needed to protect you and your loved ones.

Note: Some items may not be applicable, in which case you can leave them blank.

PERSONAL

Name (First, Middle Initial, Last Suffix):

Address:

Home #:   Work #:   Cell #:

Date of Birth:

Email address(s):

Employer & Position:

Spouse's Name (First, Middle Initial, Last Suffix):

Home #:   Work #:   Cell #:

Date of Birth:

Email address(s):

Employer & Position:

Children

1. Name: Birth Date:

2. Name: Birth Date:

3. Name: Birth Date:

4. Name: Birth Date:

THE S.M.A.R.T. ESTATE PLAN
Protecting You and Your Family

ASSETS

A. **Real Estate**: List address, current value, mortgage (if any) and how owned.

Address   *Co-owner(s)*   *Value*   *Mortgage*

1.

2.

3.

4.

B. **Bank Accounts, Investment Accounts, Retirement Accounts**

List financial institution, account type, co-ownership, and beneficiary designations.

Institution and Account Type   *Co-owner(s)*   *Value*   *Beneficiary*

1.

2.

3.

4.

5.

6.

7.

C. Antiques/Jewelry/Other Significant Personal Property

Describe the item and its approximate value.

D. Automobiles

List year, make, model, ownership, current value and loan amount, if any.

Year	Make	Model	Co-owner(s)	Value	Loan

E. Business Interests

List business name, type of business, and ownership/members.

F. Life Insurance

List each policy, number, owner, insured, beneficiary(ies), and loan, if any.

Company   Policy Type and No.   Owner   Insured Beneficiary(ies)   Loan

G. Do you currently have a Will?

YES_____NO_____

H. Do you currently have a durable financial Power of Attorney?

YES_____NO_____

I. Do you currently have a Healthcare Power of Attorney/Living Will?

YES_____NO_____

If you have any or all of these documents, please bring copies to your initial consult with trusted counsel. Additionally, please provide any documentation evidencing the assets identified above.

YOUR PLAN TO GIVE

A. Specific Gifts

Do you plan to give specific items of personal property or cash to any individual (if so, describe each gift and the recipient, including the recipient's full name and relationship to you.

Gift   *Recipient*

B. Gifts to Charity

Do you plan to give any cash or other gifts to charity (i.e. stock)?
If so, identify each charity and the specific gift.

Gift   *Recipient*

C. Real Estate

Do you want to gift real estate or interest in real estate to anyone specific?
If so, identify the real estate and recipient.

Gift   *Recipient*

D. Balance of Estate

After considering any specific gifts above, please explain how you want the balance of your estate to be distributed.

You should assume it will be converted to cash and then given to individuals.

(For example, a married couple with children may leave everything to the surviving spouse. If something happens to that spouse, then everything goes to the children).

Recipient   *Gift (specific dollar amount or percentage of remaining value)*

E. If all above-named Beneficiaries are not living...

If something happens to your spouse and children, do you want your estate to be distributed to your heirs-at-law, which means relatives per Pennsylvania law?
(The order of descent after spouse, children or their children/grandchildren is: parents, siblings, nieces or nephews, grandparents, uncles, aunts, and cousins.)
Or is there another person or entity, such as a charity that you would want to receive your assets?

Recipient   *Gift (Specific dollar amount or percentage of remaining value)*

JEFFREY L. REHMEYER II

CGA Law Firm | 717-848-4900 (office) | 717-718-7115 (direct) | jrehmeyer@cgalaw.com
www.SMARTestateplanbook.com   Page 6 of 9

217

THE S.M.A.R.T. ESTATE PLAN
Protecting You and Your Family

INDIVIDUALS UPON WHOM YOU MAY RELY

A.   **Guardian(s)** (Only necessary if any of your children are under age 18.)

A Guardian serves as the person responsible for the day-to-day upbringing of minor children in your absence. The Guardian can be a relative or friend. Some choose a married couple.

It is helpful if the Guardian(s) lives nearby, has the necessary energy to serve in a parental role, has beliefs aligned with yours, and is responsible.

Full Name and Relationship to You (first name, middle initial and last name):

Guardian:_____Co-Guardian (if any) _____

1st Alt.:_____Co-Alt. (if any) _____

2nd Alt.:_____Co-Alt. (if any) _____

B. **Trustee(s) of assets**: (Necessary if children are under age 18, but also recommended for young adults age 18-35)

A Trustee will manage money and assets on behalf of children until they are older.
The same people named as Guardian(s) can also serve as Trustee(s), if you want.
Alternatively, select a bank or trust company to serve as Trustee, which they will do for a fee.

Full Name and Relationship to You (first name, middle initial and last name):

Trustee:_____Co-Trustee (if any) _____

1st Alt.:_____Co-Alt. (if any) _____

2nd Alt.:_____Co-Alt. (if any) _____

JEFFREY L. REHMEYER II
CGA Law Firm | 717-848-4900 (office) | 717-718-7115 (direct) | jrehmeyer@cgalaw.com
www.SMARTestateplanbook.com   Page 7 of 9

218

THE S.M.A.R.T. ESTATE PLAN
Protecting You and Your Family

C. **Executor/Executrix**

This is the person who will administer your affairs as directed by your Will.
You can choose more than one person to serve as a co-executor,
but in such case, they must be able to act together.
Many name a spouse as first choice, then parents, siblings, or adult children as alternates.

Full Name and Relationship to You (first name, middle initial and last name):

Executor:_____Co-Executor (if any) _____

1st Alternate:_____Co-Alternate (if any) _____

2nd Alternate:_____Co-Alternate (if any) _____

Note: A Will does not typically address funeral or burial instructions.
That information should be provided to family or the individuals named above.
Instead, a Final Instruction Letter is used for that purpose.

D. **Power of Attorney**
This is the person(s) (your "Agent") who will make financial decisions for you if you
are unavailable or unable.

Full Name and Relationship to You (first name, middle initial and last name):

Agent:_____Co-Agent (if any) _____

1st Alternate:_____Co-Alternate (if any) _____

2nd Alternate:_____Co-Alternate (if any) _____

JEFFREY L. REHMEYER II
CGA Law Firm | 717-848-4900 (office) | 717-718-7115 (direct) | jrehmeyer@cgalaw.com
www.SMARTestateplanbook.com   Page 8 of 9

219

THE S.M.A.R.T. ESTATE PLAN
Protecting You and Your Family

E. Healthcare Power of Attorney/Living Will

This is the person you want to make medical decisions for you if you are unavailable or unable.

Full Name and Relationship to You (first name, middle initial and last name):

Agent:_____Co-Agent (if any) _____

1st Alternate:_____Co-Alternate (if any) _____

2nd Alternate:_____Co-Alternate (if any) _____

Are you or do you want to be an Organ Donor?   YES_____ NO_____

Medical considerations to discuss regarding Healthcare Power of Attorney/Living Will:

Do any of your children have special needs?

Other considerations, concerns, comments or questions regarding estate planning, family and/or assets?

Appendix C

Final Instruction Letter

This document can be used as a tool to convey key information that would be helpful upon your death. It includes information on loved ones, assets, advisors, and the location of important documents. It can also be used as a method to convey final messages to your family.

For downloadable and
printable documents visit:

www.SMARTestateplanbook.com

Protecting You and Your Family

FINAL INSTRUCTION LETTER
Funeral Arrangements

Burial _____ Cremation _____ Donated to Science _____

Funeral and/or Celebration of Life Ceremony (location and any relevant details):

Clergy (name, phone, address/email):

Funeral Director (name, phone, address/email):

I would like my body/remains placed at (location, phone/email):

In lieu of flowers, I would like contributions to (Charity, phone, address):

Persons to Notify of My Death

Name, phone, address/email

223

For the Obituary

Date and place of birth:

Parents' names and location of birth/death:

Education, graduation year, degrees earned:

Certifications, awards, other distinguishing details:

Membership in organizations, church, etc.:

For Clergy or Eulogy Speaker

Comments or information that can help paint a picture of what shaped you as a person:

(Interesting details might include family memories, your interests and hobbies, any life lessons, or your hopes and dreams to be shared with friends, family, and community.)

Helpful Professionals   (Include name, phone, address/email)

Attorney

Accountant

Financial Planner

Trust Officer

Insurance Agent

Pension Administrator

Other

Location of Important Papers

Will

Life Insurance

Health Insurance

Securities/Investments

Property Deeds

Automotive Titles

Retirement Plan [401(k), Pension, Other]

Safe Deposit Box Key

Bank, Branch Address

Business Agreements

JEFFREY L. REHMEYER II
CGA Law Firm | 717-848-4900 (office) | 717-718-7115 (direct) | jrehmeyer@cgalaw.com
www.SMARTestateplanbook.com   Page 6 of 11

227

Intentions for Children/Grandchildren

College Education (describe):

Special Training (describe):

Wedding (describe):

Arrangements for Pets

List of Major Assets for Family

Stocks, bonds, other securities
(include how registered/titled, and approximate amount and value of each)

Real Estate, Location
(include how titled, how and when acquired, estimated value,
mortgages or lines of credit, and any renter/tenant information)

JEFFREY L. REHMEYER II
CGA Law Firm | 717-848-4900 (office) | 717-718-7115 (direct) | jrehmeyer@cgalaw.com
www.SMARTestateplanbook.com   Page 8 of 11

229

Insurance Policies

(include company name, amount of policy, and beneficiaries)

Pensions/Retirement Plans/Death Benefits

(include company name, amount of plan, and beneficiaries)

Bank Accounts/Money Market/CDs, etc.

(include bank name, approximate amount, and any named beneficiaries)

Major Personal Effects, such as jewelry, furs, art, antiques or other collections
(include item, location, and approximate value)

Safe Deposit Box
(include bank location, how titled, and contents)

Liabilities *More than $2,000*

(List to whom debt is owed and the amount.)

Digital Assets (Photos, manuscripts, documents, data, cryptocurrency, videos, etc)

Social Media Accounts (Platform, username)

Location of Password List

ACKNOWLEDGMENTS

I must first thank my wife, Michele, and my family, for enriching my life substantially, every day, for years. They have taught me both the value and significance of family. I would do anything that I could to protect them.

Thanks to those who assisted me at the CGA Law Firm over the years, including the three co-founders of the Firm: Peter R. Andrews (who caused me to want to be a lawyer, was a tremendous mentor, and was always professional), Jon C. Countess (who had astounding focus and attention to detail), and Gary M. Gilbert (who was gregarious and could make a deal work between any parties). Additionally, thanks to Lawrence V. Young for exhibiting an exemplary work ethic and loving the law from the moment that I joined the Firm until this very day. Additionally, I am blessed with a number of skilled, experienced, and helpful colleagues, including phenomenal paralegals like Darlene Dubbs, Christine Garrett, Linda Miller, Barb Ross, and Tami Windholz. They have provided the kind of aid that has enabled me to focus on serving clients and developing my practice over these many years.

Thanks to Kim Walsh-Phillips and her team with Powerful Professionals, who inspired me to create the Family Matters program during which I had the opportunity to interview: Dr. Michael Spangler; Bryan Tate; Ryan Service Manzo; Jack Sommer; Scott Simonds; Mary Kay Bernosky, Esq.; Greg Nicholas; Kim Butcher; Chris Rice; and Missy Sweitzer. I value my continued relationship with them very much.

I would also like to thank my publisher, Demi Stevens, owner of Year of the Book. Her insight, creativity, guidance, and humor have been of immense value.

And finally, I would like to thank past and present clients, and welcome the ones I look forward to serving in the future. If this book can alleviate a problem or avoid some pain for at least one person, it will be worth all the work.

ABOUT THE AUTHOR

JEFFREY L. REHMEYER II is the past President of CGA Law Firm and served as the Firm's leader for nearly ten years.

Fueled by a belief that planning today creates protection for businesses and families tomorrow, Jeff forms relationships with his clients, which include large and small businesses, municipalities, families and individuals. His work begins by developing an understanding of their situation, actual or anticipated challenges, and goals.

Jeff sees the client first, not the case. From business to family to estates and individuals, he helps people realize their dreams, while protecting their rights.

www.ingramcontent.com/pod-product-compliance
Lightning Source LLC
Chambersburg PA
CBHW030503210326
41597CB00013B/778